Hard Lives,
Mean Streets

THE NORTHEASTERN SERIES ON GENDER, CRIME, AND LAW

Editor: Claire Renzetti

For a complete list of books available in this series, please visit www.upne.com

Jana L. Jasinski, Jennifer K. Wesely, James D. Wright, and Elizabeth E. Mustaine, *Hard Lives, Mean Streets: Violence in the Lives of Homeless Women*

Merry Morash, *Women on Probation and Parole: A Feminist Critique of Community Programs and Services*

Drew Humphries, *Women, Violence, and the Media: Readings in Feminist Criminology*

Gail A. Caputo, *Out in the Storm: Drug-Addicted Women Living as Shoplifters and Sex Workers*

Michael P. Johnson, *A Typology of Domestic Violence: Intimate Terrorism, Violent Resistance, and Situational Couple Violence*

Susan L. Miller, editor, *Criminal Justice Research and Practice: Diverse Voices from the Field*

Jody Raphael, *Freeing Tammy: Women, Drugs, and Incarceration*

Kathleen J. Ferraro, *Neither Angels nor Demons: Women, Crime, and Victimization*

Michelle L. Meloy, *Sex Offenses and the Men Who Commit Them: An Assessment of Sex Offenders on Probation*

Amy Neustein and Michael Lesher, *From Madness to Mutiny: Why Mothers Are Running from the Family Courts— and What Can Be Done about It*

Jody Raphael, *Listening to Olivia: Violence, Poverty, and Prostitution*

Cynthia Siemsen, *Emotional Trials: Moral Dilemmas of Women Criminal Defense Attorneys*

Lori B. Girshick, *Woman-to-Woman Sexual Violence: Stories of Women in Prison*

Karlene Faith, *The Long Prison Journey of Leslie van Houten: Life Beyond the Cult*

Jody Raphael, *Saving Bernice: Battered Women, Welfare, and Poverty*

Neil Websdale, *Policing the Poor: From Slave Plantation to Public Housing*

Lori B. Girshick, *No Safe Haven: Stories of Women in Prison*

Sandy Cook and Susanne Davies, editors, *Harsh Punishment: International Experiences of Women's Imprisonment*

Susan L. Miller, *Gender and Community Policing: Walking the Talk*

James Ptacek, *Battered Women in the Courtroom: The Power of Judicial Responses*

Neil Websdale, *Understanding Domestic Homicide*

Kimberly J. Cook, *Divided Passions: Public Opinions on Abortion and the Death Penalty*

HARD LIVES, MEAN STREETS

Violence in the Lives of Homeless Women

Jana L. Jasinski

Jennifer K. Wesely

James D. Wright

Elizabeth E. Mustaine

Northeastern University Press
Boston

Published by University Press of New England
Hanover and London

Northeastern University Press
Published by University Press of New England
One Court Street, Lebanon NH 03766
www.upne.com
© 2010 Northeastern University
All rights reserved
Manufactured in the United States of America
Designed by Katherine B. Kimball
Typeset in Scala by Integrated Publishing Solutions

University Press of New England is a member of the Green Press Initiative.
The paper used in this book meets their minimum requirement for recycled paper.

For permission to reproduce any of the material in this book, contact Permissions,
University Press of New England, One Court Street, Lebanon NH 03766;
or visit www.upne.com

Library of Congress Cataloging-in-Publication Data
Hard lives, mean streets : violence in the lives of homeless women /
Jana L. Jasinski . . . [et al.].
    p.   cm. — (The Northeastern series on gender, crime, and law)
    Includes bibliographical references and index.
    ISBN 978-1-55553-725-8 (cloth : alk. paper) — ISBN 978-1-55553-721-0
(pbk. : alk. paper)
        1. Homeless women—Violence against—United States. 2. Homeless
        women—United States—Social conditions. I. Jasinski, Jana L.
    HV4505.H367 2010
    362.83—dc22   2009047234

5   4   3   2   1

To the men and women in our study,
who let us into their lives
—the authors

To John—the adventure continues
—Jana

To the memory of my father,
Dr. Marvin L. Wesely, and to my mother,
Meridel A. Wesely, my heroes
—Jennifer

To my late and beloved brother,
Jon Kelley Wright (1959–2007):
"Our birth is nothing but
our death begun." —Edward Young
—Jim

To Mike, Kate, and Sam,
who always remind me to appreciate what I have
—Libby

When I was a child, homelessness was an old bum. A man that wanted to be called a bum, a hobo that came by and knocked on your door, said, "I'll sharpen your knives for a piece of bread." It was a man that chose to walk the tracks, put on lots of coats, and actually live, survive, and make it. Now it's a child or an unborn baby. —*Eliza*

Contents

Acknowledgments

This book would not have been possible without the support and efforts of the individuals whom we acknowledge here. First, the National Institute of Justice provided grant support that made this research possible. Special thanks to our project manager at NIJ, Dr. Leora Rosen, whose support on the administrative side was outstanding. We are also grateful to Mrs. Jean Worrall of Orlando, Florida, whose personal contacts with the shelter operators in each of the four sites we studied accomplished in a matter of days what would otherwise have taken months. Thanks also to Maggie Anderson for her help in formulating questions. Staff at the following homeless shelters across Florida assisted us with recruiting and interviewing women and men for our study: the Orlando Coalition for the Homeless, the Metropolitan Ministries in Tampa, the I. M. Sulzbacher Center for the Homeless in Jacksonville, and the Community Partnership for the Homeless, Inc., in Miami. These four facilities made our study possible, and we are pleased to acknowledge our gratitude to each of them.

A number of graduate students were involved in entering and cleaning data for this project. Rebecca Weichsel, Megan Duesterhaus, Leith Lombas, and Kristina Dzara all played a crucial role in getting the data ready for our analysis. Kimberly Murrah did an outstanding job with the transcription of the interviews.

Hard Lives,
Mean Streets

Violence, Homelessness, and Women

> The feeling of being homeless is feeling unwanted, feeling not belonging,
> feeling different. Feeling that people—you're not part of society. That you're
> separate. You live on a totally different planet. Being abused is almost the
> same feeling. The abusive want to hurt you. They want to control you.
> They look at you as a nobody, a punching bag. —*Tamara*

What we know about women who live on the street—and about their experiences with violence, both as children and as adults—is limited. Many dozens of studies of physical and sexual violence committed against homeless women have been published; comprehensive reviews of this literature include Greenan (2004), National Center on Family Homelessness (2004), and Wenzel, Leake, and Gelberg (2001). Many of these studies, however, have been more concerned with establishing the fact that violence is committed against these extremely vulnerable women than with exploring the context and experience of this violence, especially in terms of contributing risk factors, the role of violence in the etiology and dynamics of homelessness among women, or the consequences of violence in other areas of these women's lives. In short, prior research has only presented a bird's-eye view of women's experiences with violence on the street. Yet without a more complete understanding of the realities of living on the street or in a shelter, and everything that these living conditions entail, we cannot possibly hope to eliminate these experiences of violence or even design policies that might ameliorate them. The Florida Four-City Study of Violence in the Lives of Homeless Women, the results of which comprise the gist of this book, was designed to provide a more complete picture of violence in the lives of women without a home. What follows are the words and stories of more than 700 homeless women who have experienced hard lives on mean streets; we have used pseudonyms for the women we interviewed.

Virtually everyone agrees that the rates of violence against homeless women are high, measured against any standard. As Wright, Rubin, and Devine (1998, 155) note, "physical and sexual violence and exploitation are exceedingly common elements in the lives of homeless women and are, indeed, a major precipitating factor for homelessness among women." Some characteristic findings are that "women in a New York shelter were 106 times more likely to be raped, 41 times more likely to be robbed, and 15 times more likely to be assaulted than were housed African-American women" (D'Ercole and Struening 1990). Likewise, a third of the homeless women interviewed by Hilfiker (1989) reported having been raped. Wood, Valdez, Hayashi, and Shen (1990) compared homeless mothers to poor but domiciled women in Los Angeles; the homeless mothers reported more abuse by spouses than the comparison group did (35% to 16%), more childhood physical and sexual abuse (28% to 10%), and more drug use (43% to 30%) and psychiatric problems (14% to 6%). What these statistics tell us is that victimization is widespread, and that homeless women face tremendous obstacles. What they do not tell us is what these experiences mean to the women who live them every day, women like Tamara:

> I had to work. I had to go to work presentable. I couldn't go there looking like I had just slept on the street. Mentally and physically, I was stressed out. I couldn't sleep fully at night because you scared. So you sleep like with one eye open and one eye closed. You don't totally get rest. There's no way you're gonna go lay down in the street and get a full night's sleep. Because you're too scared. So every day I was fighting to keep my sanity. To go to work and be with my coworkers on a normal basis. After dealing with homeless men trying to have sex with me, trying to take my money, talking to homeless women that's talking out of they head or they mental, sleeping in the street hoping that nobody is going to come and kill me in my sleep or a rat's gonna come and bite me, and then prepare myself to look presentable, to go to work and talk on a normal average level among my coworkers and my boss, not to be sleepy, not to look drained—it was stressful.

Unfortunately Tamara's experiences are not uncommon. Wright, Devine, and Joyner (1993), for example, compared victimization experiences of homeless alcohol- and drug-impaired women in New Orleans to the experiences of homeless substance-abusive men. The average woman in that study had been robbed three times in her life, assaulted or beaten up fourteen times, raped five times, victimized by theft fourteen times, and shot at once. Overall, 90 percent of the women had experienced one or more of these events. More-recent studies report similar findings. Browne and Bassuk (1997) studied a sample of homeless women in Worcester, Massachusetts, of whom 61 percent reported having experienced severe violence at the hands of a male partner, significantly higher than the rate reported by poor but housed women in the same city. Likewise, the majority of homeless substance-abusive women studied by North, Thompson, Smith, and Kyburz (1996) acknowledged incidents of violent victimization, both as adults and as children. Similar results are reported in a number of studies since the mid-1990s (Fisher, Hovell, Hofstetter, and Hough 1995; Goodman, Dutton, and Harris 1995; North, Smith, and Spitznagel 1994; Wenzel, Koegel, and Gelberg 2000; Wenzel, Leake, and Gelberg 2001), not just in the United States but also in other nations (e.g., Breton and Bunston 1992; Charles 1994). One of the more recent and sophisticated studies in this literature is the work of Wenzel, Leake, and Gelberg (2001), who studied 974 homeless women from sixty shelters and eighteen meal programs in Los Angeles County and concluded that 34 percent of the women had experienced major violence in the year before the interview. Half the women who had experienced major violence had been assaulted at least twice. Indeed, the average homeless woman in the Los Angeles study experienced as much major violence in one year as the average American woman experiences in her entire lifetime (Wenzel, Leake, and Gelberg 2001, 746). Thus, the literature shows decisively that homeless women are victimized by violence at an elevated rate.

Still, significant issues remain. Wenzel, Leake, and Gelberg note:

> Survey research with a focus on homeless women's issues and concerns remains relatively sparse . . . Studies that have specifically examined violence against homeless women have faced limitations including small sample sizes and interview questions that have required women to label their experiences as assault. The requirement of [having to attach] such a label is less likely to reveal an episode of violence than behavioral indices that ask whether or how often certain experiences occurred. (2001, 739–40)

More generally, each study tends to use its own ad hoc measures of violence, so comparisons of results across studies are problematic. So far as we have been able to determine, for example, Wenzel, Leake, and Gelberg (2001) are the only researchers before us who have measured violence against homeless women with the Conflict Tactics Scale (Straus 1979), by far the most widely used standardized instrument in research on violence against women (National Research Council 1996, 14).

Additional problems recur throughout this literature. One is the "compared to what?" problem—that is, with which other group or groups should the victimization experiences of homeless women be compared? Several studies have no comparison group and simply report a rate or percentage for one or another sample of homeless women; here, the implicit contrast is with some ideal (but nonexistent) state in which victimization rates are zero. In some cases, homeless women are compared to homeless men (e.g., Wright, Devine, and Joyner 1993; Wenzel, Koegel, and Gelberg 2000); in others, homeless women are compared to equally poor but domiciled women (Browne and Bassuk 1997; Goodman 1991; Ingram, Corning, and Schmidt 1996); in still others, the comparison is with rates of violence against American women in general (Wenzel, Leake, and Gelberg 2001).

The reported rates of violence against homeless women, while always high, vary from study to study, at times dramatically. Published estimates of the proportion of homeless women victimized by violence vary from a low of about 30 percent to a high of about 90 percent. Part of the problem here is that different studies use different time frames (the previous six months, previous twelve months, or lifetime). Another part of the problem, as we have already stated, is the widespread use of ad hoc, unstandardized, unvalidated measurement instruments. Different studies also analyze different kinds of homeless women: some studies based on samples of single homeless women, others on samples of homeless mothers, still others on homeless women in substance abuse or mental health programs, and so on. It is possible, indeed likely, that the true rates of victimization vary sharply across subgroups (see the next section, on risk factors).

To address some of these problems, we conducted a survey of homeless women in shelters in four Florida cities (Orlando, Tampa, Jacksonville, and Miami), using the Conflict Tactics Scale (as modified by Tjaden and Thoennes 1999) as the measure of victimization experiences, obtaining both past-year and lifetime estimates of both rates and amounts of violence that these women experienced. Supplementing that quantitative survey, which we use to better understand the prevalence, risk factors, and consequences of victimization, are qualitative interviews through which emerge the voices of women whose lived experiences are rooted in complex contexts of homelessness and violence. Our research provides much-needed insight into the lives of homeless women; as we only studied women in one southern state, however, there may be geographical limitations to our findings. Our goal in this book is to present a more complete picture of the complexities of homelessness and violence as experienced by over 700 homeless women in Florida.

Risk Factors for Violent Victimization

There are multiple factors that put homeless women at risk for violent victimization. In fact, being female itself affects the types of victimization, offensive actions, and eventual justice (or lack thereof) that women experience. Unfortunately, women's experiences have often been denied or ignored in criminological research: "historically, women and girls both as victims and offenders were usually left out of the studies or, if included, were typically done so in sexist and stereotypic ways" (Belknap 2007, 2). Criminological theories were constructed around male behavior, and when researchers did begin to include female experiences, it was by using the "add women and stir" approach (Daley and Chesney-Lind 1988)—plugging girls and women into existing theories based on men's experiences. But "add women and stir" ignores how "inequalities between the sexes can differentially affect male and female experiences and behaviors" (Belknap 2007, 4). For example, Belknap (2007) points out that traditional strain theory did not measure incest as a source of strain that might lead to delinquency for either girls or boys, but after three major studies about high rates of childhood victimization for women offenders (Chesney-Lind and Rodriguez 1983; James and Meyerding 1977; Silbert and Pines 1981), many studies have identified the relationship between incest and the likelihood of adult offenses by women and men.

Research finds that girls are more likely to be sexually abused than boys. The Bureau of Justice Statistics (Snyder 2000) determined that 86 percent of all victims of sexual assault are female—including 69 percent of victims under six, 73 percent of victims under twelve, and 82 percent of victims under eighteen. Further, childhood sexual abuse significantly increases the risk of subsequent sexual and physical victimization. Noll comments:

> Thus, emerging evidence appears to suggest a persistent cycle of violence perpetrated against women that begins in childhood in the form of sexual abuse and exploitation, reemerges later in adolescence and early adulthood in

the form of physical assault/domestic violence or sexual revictimization, and ultimately places the next generation of females at considerable risk for victimization. (2005, 456).

These same patterns are evident in the data analyzed here (see chapter 6).

When examining childhood sexual abuse among the homeless, findings corroborate the gender differences described above: homeless females have experienced childhood sexual abuse at a higher rate than homeless males (Janus, Burgess, Hartman, and McCormack 1987; Whitbeck and Hoyt 1999; Whitbeck and Simmons 1990). Results from the Midwest Longitudinal Study of Homeless Adolescents indicate significantly higher rates of sexual abuse among girls (32.1%) than boys (10%; Whitbeck and Hoyt 2002), and data from the Seattle Homeless Adolescent Research and Education Project reveal that females reported higher rates (44%) of childhood sexual abuse compared to males (18%; Tyler and Cauce 2002).

Clearly, a substantial portion of homeless women have been victimized by childhood sexual abuse, and some researchers argue that childhood victimization is directly related to homelessness among adult women. In fact, whether sexual, physical, or emotional, childhood abuse is the most commonly examined risk factor in studies of girls and women who are homeless (see, e.g., Browne 1993; Browne and Bassuk 1997; Clarke, Pendry, and Kim 1997; Gilbert, El-Bassel, Schilling, and Friedman 1997; Goodman 1991; Schaff and McCane 1998; Simons and Whitbeck 1991; Wenzel, Leake, and Gelberg 2001). A study of homeless and runaway women and their experiences of early sexual abuse (Tyler, Hoyt, and Whitbeck 2000) found that exposure to childhood sexual abuse influenced the need of these girls for early independence, with few options except life on the street. Runaway girls are at higher risk for adult victimization, in part because early independence influences the channeling of homeless young females into high-risk activities like sex work (Sweet and Tewksbury 2000) or survival sex. Girls' overrepresentation as the victims of childhood sexual abuse makes them more likely than boys to run away from home for this reason, and teenage girls on the streets find few ways to survive that do not expose them to even more potential victimization.

To illustrate the general magnitude of these effects, women in the Wright, Devine, and Joyner (1993) study (based on homeless substance-abusive women in New Orleans; N = 164) who said they had been physically abused during their childhood reported more lifetime robberies (an average of 3.2 versus 1.7), "severe beatings" (10.5 versus 4.6), stabbings (0.31 to 0.14), and instances of being shot at with a gun (1.98 versus 0.23) than women who did not report childhood physical abuse. (All these differences were statistically significant.) Similar results were obtained for childhood sexual or emotional abuse. In the Wenzel, Leake, and Gelberg (2001, 745) study, logistic regression analyses showed that women who had been physically abused as children were three times more likely to have suffered major violence within the previous year than women with no history of childhood abuse. Other studies report effects of similar magnitude, and the women we interviewed were no exception. Here is the pattern as Marion describes it:

> You think somebody is supposed to love you, calm you. And starting from your childhood, all these [people] harm you: your family harm you, then your husbands harm you, your boyfriends harm you. You say, you know, there's no use to even trying to do anything. 'Cause I get up, somebody going to knock me down . . . So I started feeling like I was being used by everybody. Everybody used to taking a piece of me. You know?

In general, there is a lack of consensus as to why childhood abuse would predict adult victimization, either among homeless women or among women in general. Factors posited in the literature that link childhood abuse and adult victimization include low self-esteem, inability to maintain "normal" or "healthy" relationships, an equation among the abused between violence and love or attention, a tendency to seek out abusive relationships, lack of trust, inability to recognize the warning signs of abusive relationships, depression, and substance abuse (for an overview of the relevant literature, see Kaufman Kantor and Jasinski 1998). None of the studies cited above on the relationship between childhood and adult abuse among homeless women report multivariate analyses that even begin to specify the intervening factors in this relationship.

Consistent with the literature, Hayley's experiences of violence both during childhood and as an adult changed her behavior as well as her self-image. She states:

> I don't like to let people see me cry. I know, but see, when you're abused your whole life you don't want to let that weakness go. You know what I mean? You

don't want to let that strength down, because you don't know who's gonna take advantage of you next. And I self-mutilate myself . . . It all stems from when you're a child. Your parents breed what you are and then it's up to you to take it and go from there. And if all you are taught is bad, how you [going to] do any good?

Another commonly examined risk factor for violence against women in general is alcohol and drug abuse (see, e.g., Alexander 1996; Bennett 1995; Kilpatrick et al. 1997). Given the high rates of substance abuse characteristic of homeless populations, both male and female (on the order of 50%; see Wright, Rubin, Devine 1998), it is not surprising that this is also a risk factor for violence among homeless women (North, Thompson, Smith, and Kyburz 1996; Padgett and Struening 1992; Stein and Gelberg 1995; Steinbock 1995; Wenzel, Koegel, and Gelberg 2000; Wenzel, Leake, and Gelberg 2001). Substance abuse has been identified along with running away as "women's and girls' means of coping with and surviving abuse in their homes" (Belknap 2007, 7), thus reinforcing high-risk activities as escape options for women and girls being sexually or physically abused. It has been suggested, but not confirmed, that the relationship between substance abuse and violence is reciprocal: substance abuse increases the risk of assault (either by making homeless women more vulnerable than they would otherwise be, or by exposing them to more dangerous people and environments); assault in turn increases the rate of alcohol and drug abuse (when substances are used as coping mechanisms). Interestingly, in the Los Angeles data analyzed by Wenzel, Leake, and Gelberg, the relationship between substance abuse and violence was strong in the bivariate results but not significant in the multivariate analyses. The authors suggest (on the basis of unreported data) that trading sex is the key intervening variable (2001, 746). That is, homeless women who abuse alcohol and drugs are likely to use sex as a survival strategy, and thus are also likely to suffer violence.

Homelessness is less a condition than a process (see Wright 1988 for an early discussion of the point) and is therefore not "of a piece." Homeless women (and men) vary dramatically in the length, conditions, nature, and severity of their homelessness, and these variations also represent plausible risk factors for violence among homeless women (Geissler et al. 1995; Wenzel, Leake, and Gelberg 2001). Some homeless women have only recently become homeless, while others have been homeless for decades. The obvious hypothesis—the more time on the street, the higher the odds of violent victimization (or the greater the amount of violence experienced)—has received some support in the few studies that have examined such factors (see the two studies just cited). Likewise, some women have experienced just one or two episodes of homelessness in their lifetimes, while others have experienced many; "a greater number of distinct lifetime episodes of homelessness . . . predicted experience of major violence" in the only study we know of that has examined this factor (Wenzel, Leake, and Gelberg 2001, 746). It is also plausible that homeless women who frequent high-crime areas within their cities (so-called hot spots) experience more violence than other homeless women; this seems to be true in the general population (Rodgers and Roberts 1995) and may also be true for homeless women (North, Smith, and Spitznagel 1994).

Scholars familiar with the literature on homelessness might further hypothesize about connections between aspects of homelessness and violence committed against homeless women. Some homeless women spend most of their nights in shelters; others sleep in the streets. It is an obvious guess that the latter experience more violence than the former. (See chapter 5 for our analyses of lifestyle factors and their relationship to victimization.) Homeless women with dependent children may have different experiences with violence than lone homeless women. Homeless women with male partners (husbands, boyfriends, or simply companions) may profit from male guardianship or suffer from proximity to potentially abusive men. Salomon, Bassuk, and Huntington (2002) found that 62 percent of the poor and homeless women they studied had a history of physical violence at the hands of male partners. Although lifestyle explanations of victimization can be a useful tool for understanding how homelessness impacts the risk of violent victimization, with the addition of feminism, these explanations can be seen against the background of societal norms and values about violence against women, and can provide a more complete understanding of these risks (Schwartz and Pitts 1995). Dynamics of power and control, at the crux of violence against women, feed directly into a context in which many victimized, poor women teeter at the edge of homelessness. In *Saving Bernice: Battered Women, Welfare and Poverty*, Raphael (2000) documents the extent to which abusers sabotage the attempts of low-income women to improve the conditions of their lives. She finds that the women's partners thwart their efforts to get job training, education, or professional skills; arrange child care; or find transportation: "welfare benefits alone are also too low in the United States to enable women to have the economic wherewithal to escape violence and support themselves and their children" (112). What alternatives remain?

One of the fundamental results of research on homelessness in the 1980s and 1990s was the demonstration that much homelessness is not chronic (Wright 1988). Some people, once they become homeless, do tend to stay homeless more or less indefinitely, but most homelessness is either episodic (episodically homeless people cycle regularly through episodes of homelessness punctuated by periods of more or less stable housing circumstances) or transitional (single episodes of homelessness that are quickly resolved). One might assume that chronically homeless women suffer more continuous exposure to risk and would therefore be victimized at higher rates (or suffer more aggregate violence). On the other hand, the housing circumstances through which episodically and transitionally homeless women cycle are obviously not stable and may not be particularly functional—in fact, it is possible that these households are characterized by high levels of intimate partner violence. This reinforces the likelihood, mentioned above, that the experience of violence is a factor contributing to the cycle of homelessness among women, a common (but largely untested) assumption.

One important way in which homeless women differ among themselves is in what they do to survive life on the streets. The effects of various kinds of survival strategies on the experience of violence have been examined mainly among samples of homeless and runaway youth (Tyler, Hoyt, and Whitbeck 2000; Tyler, Hoyt, Whitbeck, and Cauce 2001) and to a much lesser extent on homeless women in general (Wenzel, Koegel, and Gelberg 2000; Wenzel, Leake, and Gelberg 2001). One high-risk activity is panhandling. Some homeless women deal drugs in order to survive; in the Wright, Devine, and Joyner study (1993), those who did had higher rates of lifetime violence victimization than those who did not. Trading sex for money, shelter, or drugs has been documented as a risk factor for violence in all relevant studies of homeless women. Survival strategies like sex work and survival sex can overlap; over half the women in a u.s. survey considered their pimp to be their boyfriend at the time they were recruited into the prostitution industry (Hynes and Raymond 2002) Street prostitution is highly dangerous. According to Raphael, more than twenty research studies have documented an "almost unimaginable level of violence in street prostitution" (2004, 100). This is illustrated by the case study of Olivia (Raphael 2004), a former street prostitute who states that out of fifteen customers a night, about half would perpetrate violence in the form of physical beatings, attacks, and rapes, as well as degrading verbal attacks. Clearly, prostitution and other survival strategies (panhandling, drug dealing, and the like) increase homeless women's exposure to violence.

Other possible risk factors for violence against homeless women include mental illness, criminal histories, and various demographic factors such as age or race. Roughly one-third of the homeless have significant psychiatric impairments; the rate of mental illness is higher among homeless women than among homeless men (Wright, Rubin, and Devine 1998). One supposes that mentally ill homeless women are more vulnerable across the board than other homeless women, and that they would therefore suffer more violence. About a quarter of homeless people (both men and women) have prior felony convictions (most for drug offenses; again, see Wright, Rubin, and Devine 1998). Whether those who do are victimized at higher rates than those who do not is an unresearched issue. The effect of race on violence against homeless women has been investigated, but the results are inconclusive: in some studies, homeless women of color experience higher rates of violence, but in other studies, the opposite is true. The general effects of age on victimization are unknown, although studies of young homeless and runaway girls report rampant victimization.

Structural explanations of victimization among homeless individuals focus on the external forces increasing risk. According to the "routine activities/lifestyles" theory, victimization (violent or otherwise) results from the lifestyles or daily routines of individuals (see, e.g., Cohen and Felson 1979; Hindelang, Gottfreson, and Garofalo 1978; Mustaine and Tewksbury 1997a). The routine activities theory has three prerequisites: the presence of a motivated offender, the absence of effective guardians, and the availability of suitable targets. Daily routines thus influence exposure to potential offenders, the victim's value or vulnerability as a target, and the presence or absence of guardians capable of affording protection. The key insight of the theory is that social context is central in predicting victimization. Lee and Schreck (2005) argue that the marginality of homeless individuals and their consequent lifestyle exposes them to victimization. It is hard to imagine a lifestyle or set of routine daily activities more conducive to victimization than homelessness. Homeless people, both male and female, spend their days and nights in run-down areas of cities—areas where potential offenders are numerous, and where exposure to the risk of violence is an everyday occurrence. Further, they do not have the protection and safety of permanent housing; they often carry most, if not all, of their belongings with them. High rates of substance abuse and psychiatric impairment and long stretches of homelessness also increase vulnerability and impair guardianship.

These issues become more nuanced when the gendered context is considered, and it is here that a feminist routine activities theoretical framework may be useful in understanding women's risk of violent victimization (Schwartz, DeKeseredy, Tait, and Alvi 2001; Schwartz and Pitts 1995). It is well documented that females are much more likely to be victims of sexual assault than males (Belknap 2007). Though research finds that violence against women in the private realm exceeds that in the public sphere (Dobash and Dobash 1992; Hollander 2001), fears of sexual victimization are reinforced by daily experiences that expose homeless women to high levels of vulnerability and risk. The "routine activities/lifestyles" theories may thus provide a plausible conceptual schematic for research on this topic. As society's throwaways, the homeless are objects of contempt, fear, and distaste. This ensures that no one intervenes to protect them (through formal or informal mechanisms) or punish those who violate them. Further, societal norms tacitly accepting violence against the homeless increase homeless women's risk of violent victimization (Schwartz and Pitts 1995). Vulnerable populations like homeless women are easily targeted.

Violence as a Cause of Homelessness among Women

The "Domestic Violence and Homelessness" fact sheet published by the National Coalition for the Homeless (2008) cites domestic violence as a "contributing factor" to homelessness among women. Research tends to support this finding. In a study of 777 homeless parents in ten cities, 22 percent reported leaving their last residence because of domestic violence (Homes for the Homeless 1998). Likewise, a Minnesota study (Wilder Research Center 1998) found that 19 percent of homeless women mentioned abuse as one of the main reasons they were homeless; the corresponding figure in a Missouri study was 18 percent (De Simone, Gould, and Stretch 1998). Other pertinent studies showing similar results include Bufkin and Bray (1998); Clarke, Pendry, and Kim (1997); Kannah et al. (1992); Metraux and Culhane (1999); and North, Thompson, Smith, and Kyburz (1996). Results from these studies tend to converge on about one in five as the proportion of homeless women who report violence or abuse as the (or one) reason why they are homeless. (This is an estimate of how many women are homeless because of an immediately prior episode of intimate partner violence. It is not an estimate of how many homeless women have ever experienced such episodes, which would certainly be a much greater proportion.) Since violence against women is highly underreported, the true proportion may be much higher.

Complicating the numbers is the potential role that violence against women in the home might play in the cycle of episodic homelessness to which we alluded earlier, the process by which many women move into and out of homelessness. One possible pattern is that women flee abuse and thereby become homeless. Later, a desperate need for safety, protection, or basic necessities for herself (and often her children)—perhaps combined with the abuser's pleas, promises, and apologies—may lead to a woman's temporary reconciliation with her partner, and to another cycle of abuse-homelessness-reconciliation at a later date. Another possible pattern is that women are abused, escape to homelessness, and eventually link up with a new male partner who is also abusive.

Consequences of Violence

Compared to the other areas of research already reviewed, the literature on what happens to homeless women in the aftermath of violent victimization is minuscule but intriguing. Several studies (Browne 1993; Goodman and Dutton 1996; Goodman, Dutton, and Harris 1997) find that victimization exacerbates psychiatric symptoms, chiefly depression and anxiety—a common response to violence among all women, whether homeless or not (Giles-Sims 1998). One study (Browne, Salomon, and Bassuk 1999) has examined "the impact of recent partner violence on poor women's capacity to maintain work." Controlling for various factors, the result was that poor women who did not experience major partner violence in the previous year were three times more likely than women who did to work at least 30 hours per week in the subsequent six-month period. Raphael (2000) finds clear relationships between intimate partner violence and poverty, largely due to the abuser's tactics of sabotage, threats, and violence that keep the victim trapped and unable to work for any length of time despite her multiple attempts to do so:

> Welfare-to-work and job training providers around the country report similar stories of education- and work-related sabotage. Women's partners tear up books and homework assignments, rip clothing and winter coats, and inflict visible bruises to prevent the women from attending class. Promising to drive the women to classes or work, their partners consistently bring them late in the hopes that they will be dismissed. (32)

Baker, Cook, and Norris (2003) argue that these coercive and controlling tactics by abusers put women in situations in which they are faced with losing welfare benefits because they cannot meet the work requirements. Yet working puts them at risk for abuse by their partners. Consequently, women who are abused and poor may find themselves only one step away from homelessness. Women who are able to leave their abusers find their financial situation even more challenging, as their choice is between violent victimization and being without a home.

There is also limited evidence that episodes of violence compromise the efficacy of substance abuse treatment among alcoholic and drug-addicted homeless women (North, Thompson, Smith, and Kyburz 1996). And one Ph.D. dissertation suggests that violence against homeless mothers negatively affects their parenting skills (Lindsay-Blue 1999), as it affects the parenting skills of abused women in general (Wolak and Finkelhor 1998).

One obvious problem in sorting out the effects of violence on homeless women is that many of the outcome variables one would want to examine are also risk factors for violence, and the cross-sectional surveys that predominate in this literature make it difficult to separate causes from effects. Longitudinal research over years or decades would be ideal, but that lies beyond the scope of the present study. We were able, however, to identify specific recent experiences with violence in the lives of the women we studied (both violence in their former homes and general neighborhood or community violence), and to ask them about what happened to them or what they felt immediately after those experiences. Retrospective research of this sort, while falling short of true longitudinal research, at least allows us to identify the temporal ordering of events and to generate potentially interesting causal hypotheses.

Criminal Justice Response

As homeless women navigate experiences of past or current violence while also engaging in survival strategies that may put them at even greater risk, there are opportunities for intervention in their lives that are being missed. It is likely that at least some women become homeless because of how the criminal justice system deals (or does not deal) with violent victimization in their homes. This was true for Eliza, who recalled:

> In the neighborhood that I grew up in, it was nothing to see a woman dragged, knocked down, stomped, and beat. And there was no safe house, there was no Harbor House, there was no shelter that a wife or a woman could run to and really be protected, shielded, and safe. So, many women—the women that I knew, including my mother—they stood there and they took it. And if the police were called, they were so friendly and familiar with the people in the neighborhood, they would kind of pat the man or—in other words, "keep it down." So there was no safety zone. I've seen some women escape by getting on a Greyhound [bus] in Pittsburgh and splitting. But I saw a lot of women die as a result of being abused.

Most studies of violence against homeless women have discussed the implications of their results for care providers or for the police, but none, so far, have asked samples of victimized homeless women whether their victimizations were reported to the authorities and, if so, with what effects or results. Adding the standard reporting questions from the criminal victimization surveys to a survey of violence as experienced by homeless women, as we have done, does not by any means constitute the last word on the issue; rather, it constitutes the first.

Conclusions

Our review of the literature indicates that little research has focused on the experiences of violence in the lives of homeless women, and that what does exist reaches no clear conclusions about what factors might increase or decrease victimization risk, the consequences of this violence, or interactions with the criminal justice system. This study, although still exploratory, has as its primary goal developing an understanding of the role of violence in the lives of homeless women. The objectives are to determine how many women have experienced some form of violence in their lives either as children or adults, what factors are associated with experiences of violence, what are the consequences of violence, and which types of interactions occur with the justice system. Further, our qualitative work gives voice to the numbers and provides context that is missing from much of the research on the vulnerability of homeless women.

We hypothesized that the majority of the women in our sample would tell us that they had experienced some type of violence as children or adults. The use of standardized measures that have previously been utilized with community samples allows us to make comparisons between our sample of homeless individuals and other community samples. Based upon the literature discussing risk factors for violence in community samples, we hypothesized that these same factors would be associated with increased risk for victimization among our sample of homeless individuals. These factors include childhood victimization (of any type), substance abuse, and demographic factors. Because we know that being homeless is different from being housed, we also hypothesized that some factors related to being homeless would be associated with violence victimization. Using a gendered lens to engage the theoretical framework of the routine activities theory, we hypothesized that characteristics of homelessness (e.g., number of times homeless, length of time homeless, locations in which time is spent) would be associated with victimization.

Each of the topics discussed above provides new information to help us understand the complexities of hard lives and mean streets.

2

Study Participants: Florida's Homeless Women

I'm not gonna say it's sad, but I still have a lot of issues that I haven't learned to let go yet. I used to take counseling years ago, but I quit because I thought I was a tough guy but I guess I'm not. That's why I work a lot because when I work it keeps my mind occupied. I work and I work very well . . . I just have issues that I need to deal with, and I can't do it on my own. —*Rena*

Rena, thirty-nine years old, had been living in the Orlando homeless shelter for about a month when we interviewed her. This was the most recent in a long series of homelessness episodes that began when she was about sixteen. She said this about her current stint in the shelter:

I didn't want to come here—to me this is rock bottom. I don't have my place anymore; I'm in a shelter. This is *rock bottom*. So what's next? I gotta do what I gotta do to make it better. This year has got to be my year.

As it unfolded, her narrative detailed a stark, unending landscape of violence and misery. Such lived experiences amply illustrate a number of the key themes that we develop in this book. Her story, then, is an appropriate way to begin a discussion about the women in this study.

At three months of age, Rena was brought to the mainland United States from Puerto Rico to be raised by her grandparents because her father abused drugs, her, and her mother. When we asked about being separated from her parents at an early age, Rena explained:

It was because of my dad being abusive to my mom and because of drug abuse. My dad's been using drugs all my life. That's where I get it from. My dad was using when my mother had me. And he was abusive with her while she was pregnant with me. So my mother tried to kill me when I was a little girl. She didn't want me because of my dad.

Rena's experiences with violence date back to her earliest childhood memories. Her history of sexual abuse is more recent: it dates to the third grade. She was, in her words, "a pretty little girl" who was an obvious target for men who "you know, got to thrive on little girls."

I went to school here at Grand Avenue Elementary School. That's where I got raped the first time—I got raped in the third grade. The janitor raped me in the school bathroom.

Rena recalls her grandparents as capable and loving surrogate parents. When told about the rape, her grandmother went to the school armed with a shotgun to confront the rapist—she "went there to blow his brains out"— but he had left for the day and died of natural causes a few years later.

The third-grade rape was the first of several. Her first experience with forced oral sex, when she was fourteen, happened five doors down from the house where she lived with her grandparents. She had gone with her sister to a birthday party, and when the sister left with some men, three other men took Rena upstairs to the bathroom, and "all three of them raped me at one time."

Then in her early twenties, during a visit to her cousin, she was sexually attacked by a man with a knife:

He took me to the school over there and raped me for over two hours. I had whips [sic] all around my neck from the knife. If I would have retaliated, I would have been dead, because another girlfriend of mine, she lived in the same building, and they found her in the same park with her throat cut the very next night. I believe that was meant for me. But by me doing what the guy wanted me to do, that saved my life—plus I was praying all the same time he was on top of me, praying to God, "Lord please don't let him kill me." And he finally let me go.

Rena described several more rapes during the interview, and at one point was asked how the seemingly relentless sexual assaults made her feel:

Nasty. When I got raped, I felt like shit. I felt like shit and I felt like, "Why me?"
I was mad with the Lord. I would say, "Why me, why me, why me?" With all
these women running around giving it away free, why me? So that's when
[I started], you know, the drugs, the alcohol.

Rena's grandmother died when Rena was sixteen, and she has been on
her own ever since. Her strengths in school were athletics and music, but
academically, she had problems and was placed in what she describes as
"slow learner classes." She left school at eighteen for a short-lived marriage
to an abusive man:

He used to lock me in a trailer, used to jump on me, and he was just abusive.
When I got saved, he told me I was going to church too much and that I was
sleeping with the preacher! It was just stupid. [Question: And you were with
him for how long?] Six, seven months. Before he got killed.

We asked for details, only to learn that Rena's husband was shot in the
head and back with a shotgun by the husband of the woman he was seeing
on the side. This was Rena's only marriage, and she has no children. After
her husband's murder, she had several female lovers. Most of them were
abusive, too. She described one instance involving an older female lover
who "beat the crap out of me with a stick" and told numerous other stories
of injury, assault, and violence.

When asked, "Have you ever been violent towards anyone?" Rena responded, "Very much so." A great deal of Rena's own perpetration of violence involved partners and drugs:

I would work hard for my money, come home, find my woman doing drugs,
and they shot their mouths off, and I'd go off. I mean, I'm working hard, my girlfriend's home doing drugs all day with her friends, and I'd go off, go in a damn
rage . . . I got pissed, in other words, and you know, I broke her arm twice. I've
been very abusive. I'm not gonna lie, I mean, I've been very abusive.

Rena's violent rages have landed her in prison three times, once for
arson, once for aggravated assault with a firearm, and once for attempted
murder. The arson charge resulted from a girlfriend who was using Rena's
money to smoke crack:

She told me, "I want you to get out." I said, "OK, I'll get out." So I took some lighter fluid—you know, what you use to light the barbeque. I was not high. I was just mad, angry. All my inner anger just came out of me. And I took the lighter fluid and I poured it all over the house. I poured it all over the house and then struck a match to it and it went up—the whole house was on fire within two seconds. [Snaps her fingers.] It was just like that. And I walked out.

The attempted murder charge also involved an ex-girlfriend, who had lied about Rena's sexual involvement with another woman. Rena asserts that this was not a murder attempt in earnest. Apparently, the judge agreed, because she did only two months in prison, participated in mandatory counseling, and was then released for time served.

In and out of prison, in and out of abusive and failed relationships, a history of failed suicide attempts, and in and out of homelessness. Rena has been homeless "on and off" since she was sixteen, and when asked about the number of homeless episodes, she responded: "oh man, six, seven. More?" And why? "It's been alcohol and drugs, or my financial situation with my job, and well, you know, one thing after another." Here is a characteristic and telling interview sequence:

Interviewer: And what were the causes of your being homeless for these periods of time?

Rena: I can say relationships, drinking and drugs with them, and, you know, me trying to do the right thing, but it makes me relapse when I'm around people who continue to do it.

Interviewer: So was it because of the drinking and the drugs in the relationship or was it the violence in the relationship?

Rena: That too.

Interviewer: Would you be homeless with your girlfriend or boyfriend at the time?

Rena: Just me.

Interviewer: Just you? Like when you'd leave them?

Rena: Yeah, I'd be living with them. Yeah.

Interviewer: So, you'd be living with them and you'd leave them and then—

Rena: Or they would put me out.

Interviewer: Okay. And then where would you stay when that would happen?

Rena: On the street . . . in the park. I slept in cars and different places with different people on different nights. Mostly it's been with different friends. And crack houses. I don't approve of crack houses because if you are trying to stay clean and you're living in a crack house, there's no way in hell you gonna stay clean.

As these comments suggest, drugs and alcohol have been present throughout Rena's life: "I've been doing drugs for a long time. Crack and drinking and drugging. I been drinking since I was little. I don't smoke weed. I drink like hell though!" Her father was a drug abuser, as have been most of her friends and lovers along the way. "But my biggest thing right now is not drugs, it's my drinking. It's my drinking, it is. If it was drugs, I wouldn't be sitting here talking to you. I'd be out smoking right now. I'd say okay, well, bye. Give me my things and I'm out of here."

Rena notes that instead of being at the homeless shelter, she could be surviving by prostituting herself, selling drugs, or stealing. By portraying these as options, but ones she sees as less appealing than the shelter, she constructs her stay at the homeless center as a choice she is making to better herself. Early in the interview, she stated:

If I want to do the right thing, then I got to stay where I'm at. Nobody has to be homeless. I mean, we females. A female never has to worry about a place to stay. But I'm not gonna get out there and get on a block [become a prostitute; find a block where no prostitute is working, and turn tricks there] or go rob somebody or have oral sex with some man or have this other man dropping it down on my guts [having sex with me]. I'd rather be right here where I'm at and put up with it, and deal with it than to put up with that.

And toward the end of the interview, she said:

I'm telling you, I could be out there slinging drugs right now. I could be out there robbing somebody. I could be out there selling weed, stealing clothes. There's a lot of things I could be doing besides being [at this shelter]. So obviously, it's something I want to do right. I'm sitting here. I'm in this shelter. Because we all have choices, but it depends on what kind of choices you make.

At the homeless shelter, Rena seems dedicated to the goal of improving her life, attending meetings of Alcoholics Anonymous and Narcotics Anonymous, keeping up with her mental-health counseling sessions, meeting with her case manager, attending church every so often, doing construction work at the nearby day labor outlet, and "just trying to make the best out of the program." Although she struggles with low self-esteem and depression, she sees herself as a hard-working woman with a decent chance at success. She concluded her interview with this observation:

> Hell, it could be worse. I could be dead on top of being homeless. But I don't want to be like this all my life. Being a female, I don't want to keep going through the cycle. I just don't want to be like this so I'm gonna take this [program] and do what I got to do with it . . . It just make me sit back and say, do I want to be like this for the rest of my life?

Rena is one of over 700 women who were participants in a multisite, multi-year study of violence in the lives of homeless women. Her story, as we have said, illustrates in meaningful human terms a large number of key themes that emerged during the course of our work. Just how her life story relates to that of the average woman in our study is the topic we consider next.

The Demographics and Histories of Homeless Women

The Florida study was designed to elicit as much information as possible about homeless women's experiences with violence, while using standardized measurement tools so the results would be comparable to research on housed women. Recognizing that the use of such standardized instruments might potentially reduce the richness of the information we received, we supplemented the survey with qualitative interviews that resulted in many narratives not unlike Rena's. Together, these various sources of information provide a very complete and detailed portrait of what these women dealt with on a day-to-day basis, the backgrounds of their homelessness, and their experiences with violence in many forms.

The current chapter goes on to summarize the demographic composition of the sample, discuss their families of origin and early life experiences, review issues of behavioral health (addictions and mental illness), and present their homelessness histories. The women's adult experiences with violence, as both victims and perpetrators; their encounters with the criminal justice system; their day-to-day lives; and the consequences of all this for their outlooks and self-esteem are discussed in subsequent chapters.

One component of our study that this and subsequent chapters do not discuss in depth is the technical details about how the survey, interviews, and focus group were conducted, how sampling was done, how interviewers were trained, and so on. It is important that readers have access to these methodological details, but they do not make for very interesting reading. So we have placed the technical material in an appendix that readers may consult at their leisure. Here we simply provide a description of the over 700 homeless Florida women who participated in the study. Our aims are to introduce the women to the reader, and to assure readers that the women we studied are similar in most respects to homeless women throughout the United States.

The best available data on "homeless women throughout the United States" is the National Survey of Homeless Assistance Providers and Clients (NSHAPC), conducted by Martha Burt and her associates in 1996 (Burt, Aron, and Lee 2001). Although now more than a decade old, the NSHAPC remains the closest thing we have to a national sample of homeless people. Wherever possible, we have compared our sample to the female respondents in the NSHAPC, to illustrate both similarities and differences between homeless women in Florida and those in the nation at large.

DEMOGRAPHIC BACKGROUNDS

Education. Rena described herself as a slow learner and left school without a diploma at eighteen. In these respects, she resembles the stereotype of a homeless person more than the reality. Virtually every study of homeless people undertaken in the past three decades has reported that the homeless are "surprisingly" well educated, and our study is no exception. Nearly two-thirds of the women in our quantitative sample had a high school degree, and more than a third had additional education. Although these numbers lag behind those for the Florida population as a whole (80% of whom in the 2000 U.S. Census had a high school degree, and 51% of whom had additional education), they exceed the levels of educational attainment reported for Burt's homeless women (56% of whom had a high school diploma or more; Burt, Aron, and Lee 2001). Given the level of impoverishment characteristic of homeless women, they prove to be a rather well-educated group, a fact worth bearing in mind when "more education" is suggested as a solution to the problems of the homeless.

Among the qualitative interviewees, all but two either had some high school education, were working on their GED, had completed high school, or had earned their GED. Of the two exceptions, one was illiterate, and the other had an associate's degree. Thus on average, the participants in our quantitative and qualitative samples resemble homeless women in general.

Racial and Ethnic Makeup. Rena is of mixed ethnicity, though she identifies her race as black (when asked "And your race is?" she answered: "I'm mixed. Well, I'm Puerto Rican and black but I always put black down. My mother is mixed and my daddy is black."). So do almost half of the homeless women in our sample (47% identified themselves as black or African American). White women comprised one-third of the sample, followed by Hispanic or Latina women (15%). In most studies (including ours), respondents can identify themselves as white, black, or Hispanic; in the U.S. Census, Hispanics can be of any race (ie., race and Hispanic status are asked as separate questions, precisely because of people like Rena). Thus, precise comparisons between our results and those of the census cannot be made. In the 2000 census, however, only 15 percent of Floridians were identified as African American, so that group is heavily overrepresented in our sample of homeless women, as, indeed, is the case in nearly every study of U.S. homelessness (e.g., Burt, Aron, and Lee 2001; Hopper 2003; Kusmer 2002). In the NSHAPC, 34 percent of women with children were white, 45 percent were African American, and 16 percent were Hispanics (with the remainder in other categories), virtually identical to the Florida women.

Among the qualitative interviewees were six African American women, three Hispanic women, one African American and American Indian woman, one Puerto Rican and black woman (Rena), and nine white women.

While it is true that homelessness among both men and women transcends race (also gender, age, and other demographic characteristics), it is also undeniably true that racial minorities are grossly overrepresented among the nation's homeless (Asians being the only exception). Thus, part of the explanation for the rapid growth of homelessness in American cities since the early 1980s must be found in systematic discrimination against nonwhites. Interestingly, even when socioeconomic status is controlled for, African Americans worry far more than whites about hunger and homelessness, according to a March 2005 Gallup poll (Lyons 2005).

Marital Status and Fertility. Lack of familial ties and profound estrangement from kith and kin are widely understood to be among the distinguishing marks of homeless people and a principal reason why people become homeless in the first place (see, e.g., Wright, Rubin, and Devine 1998). They are also risk factors for violent victimization and potential barriers to help seeking.

Consistent with this understanding, 83 percent of the women in our study had either never married (43%) or, like Rena, were divorced, separated from their spouses, or widowed (40%). Only about one in six of the women was married or cohabiting at the time of the interview. The women in the NSHAPC were nearly identical: 46 percent never married, 39 percent divorced and separated, and 15 percent currently married or cohabiting. By way of contrast, in 2003, only 24 percent of the U.S. adult population had never married; 59 percent were currently married, and only 10 percent were separated or divorced. Thus, stable marital relationships are much rarer among homeless women than in the population at large.

Among the women in our sample who had been married, the average number of marriages was 1.4. Thus, the majority of the ever-married, like Rena, married only once; about 40 percent married a second time, and a few were on their third or fourth marriages. (Unfortunately, the data in Burt, Aron, and Lee 2001 refer only to current marriages, not marital histories.) Most of the women we interviewed (80%), regardless of their past or present marital status, had one or more children, and the average number of children was 2.39. In Burt, Aron, and Lee's national data—also regardless of past or present marital status—76 percent of the women, but only 57 percent of the men, had one or more children, nearly identical to the Florida results. Finally, the women in our study who had ever given birth were relatively young when they first did so (the average age at first birth was 19.8 years); however, one in three women gave birth before they turned eighteen. In the United States as a whole, women's average age at first birth has been steadily increasing for the last thirty years; in 2002, about the time our survey was being conducted, it reached an all-time high of 25.1 years (Centers for Disease Control 2005).

In subsequent research at the Orlando site, we inquired about the fertility histories of all the women in the shelter, regardless of whether they had children with them or not (Dotson 2009). Interestingly, among women who were in the shelter as "single" women (i.e., there without children), one in three (33.2%) in fact had children from whom they were separated. And among women who were in the shelter with one or more children in their care, one in four (24.8%) also had other children from whom they were separated. In some cases, the absent children had been taken from their mothers by the Florida Department of Children and Families; in other cases, the mothers saw an episode of homelessness coming and left their children with relatives, friends, or other caretakers while they weathered the storm. In more than a few cases, these women were separated or estranged from their children because of issues involving intimate partner violence, child abuse or neglect, and similar factors.

The marital status and family backgrounds of the qualitative interviewees should be considered in light of the fact that all participants had experienced some form of violence, which is not necessarily true either of our complete Florida sample or of Burt, Aron, and Lee's national sample. All but two of the women told us that they had been victimized by intimate partners. As a result, their intimate relationship patterns were chaotic. Altogether, seven were divorced or separated, nine were single, two were presently married, and two were widowed. Fifteen of the women had children, and seven of those with children had had one or more of their children removed from their homes, either by family members or by child protective services. The same is true of about two in five of the women in Burt, Aron, and Lee's sample who had at least one minor child (2001, 141; see also Dotson 2009). Burt, Aron, and Lee eloquently summarize the plight faced by the children of homeless women: "These children are caught between two very undesirable alternatives—either they share their mother's homelessness, or they run a high risk of being placed in foster care. Each is well-known to have serious negative consequences" (2001, 158).

The in-depth nature of the qualitative interviews revealed the ambiguous and overlapping nature of these categories. For instance, one widow lost a husband of fourteen years but subsequently acquired an abusive boyfriend. Many of those who described themselves as single had boyfriends or on-again, off-again partners, many of whom were abusive. As has been pointed out for decades (see, e.g., Stack 1974), marriage and kinship terms as they are understood in white, middle-class communities often do not adequately describe the experiences of poor African American women, among whom marital and marriage-like relationships are far more fluid and informal than commonly used kinship terms suggest.

Age. Part of the stereotype of homeless people is that they are old, broken-down alcoholics and bag ladies, but nearly every study reports the average age of the homeless to be in the thirties. The average age of the women in our sample is 37.5 years, similar to the average age of women in Burt, Aron, and Lee's data and to Rena, who was thirty-nine when we interviewed her. Twenty-eight percent of the women in our study are under 30 (identical to the NSHAPC figure), 47 percent are between thirty and forty-five (42% in the NSHAPC), 24 percent are between forty-six and sixty-four (23% in the NSHAPC), and fewer than 1 percent are older (6% in the NSAPC).

Other than the relatively low average age, the most surprising thing about the age distribution (in our and all other samples of the homeless) is the underrepresentation of the elderly. In the U.S. population, 12.4 percent are sixty-five or older. In samples of the homeless, despite the stereotype, rarely are more than 4 percent over sixty-five (Wright, Donley, and Dietz 2008). A similar deficit of elderly homeless has also been reported in Canada (Stergiopoulos and Herrmann 2003).

Why are the elderly homeless comparatively rare? Two hypotheses have been suggested (Wright, Donley, and Dietz 2008). First, a range of benefit programs become available to people once they turn sixty-five (among which Social Security, Medicare, and various housing subsidies are the most important); these programs may be sufficient in many instances to get homeless people off the streets, or to allow aging poor people to avoid homelessness. A second and more troubling hypothesis is that homeless people rarely survive to old age. Roughly a dozen studies of mortality among the homeless have been published, and the common finding is that the average age at death is somewhere in the early fifties (see O'Connell 2005 for a review). It is likely that both these hypotheses are true.

Geographic Origins. That the homeless are from somewhere else, and thus are somebody else's problem, has become an article of faith in discussions of public policy. In fact, research shows that the geographic origins of homeless people tend to mirror those of the area's nonhomeless population—that is, areas with high in-migration in general also tend to have large proportions of their homeless population who migrated in from elsewhere, while areas with low in-migration in general also have low in-migration among the homeless. In a state such as Florida, then, we would expect a fairly large fraction of the state's homeless to have originated in other states, or other countries.

In 2006, Florida's population was estimated to be about 18.1 million, of whom 3.4 million (18.8%) were foreign born. Among the homeless women in our sample, 12.1 percent were foreign born, substantially lower than the figure for the state population as a whole. Of the state's 3.4 million foreign-born residents, 47 percent are naturalized US citizens. Among the 89 foreign-born homeless women in our study, 56 (or 63) are naturalized citizens. (In addition, 28% are resident aliens, 3% are in the United States on temporary visas, and 6% are illegal immigrants.) Taking both the native-born and naturalized citizens together, 96 percent of the homeless women in our sample are u.s. citizens, slightly higher than the statewide figure. Among the women in our sample born outside the fifty states, the largest group is from Puerto Rico (21%), followed by Cuba (16%) and other Central and South American countries (19%). The remaining women come from a wide variety of European, Asian, and African countries.

Among the native-born women in our sample (N = 648), the single largest group was born in Florida (36%); in fact, one in four of the women was born in the same metropolitan area where they were interviewed. Forty-three percent of Florida's native-born population was born in the state. So while the state's homeless women are somewhat less likely than Floridians as a whole to be born abroad, they are somewhat more likely to have been born in a different state. As a result, 32 percent of the sample of homeless women were born in Florida, while 34 percent of Floridians overall were born in the state—virtually identical figures. In other words, homeless women in Florida are not any more transient than the state's general population.

Again, Rena is a good example. Born in Puerto Rico, she was brought to Florida to live with her grandparents before she was a year old, and she has been an Orlando resident ever since.

U.S. regions outside of Florida that contribute noticeably large numbers to the homeless women's sample include the New York–New Jersey area (97 women), the Midwest (Illinois, Indiana, Michigan, and Ohio—67 women), and nearby southeastern states (Georgia, Alabama, Mississippi, South and

North Carolina, and Virginia—88 women). Although comparable state-wide data have not been located, it is a very good bet that these are the same states from whence large numbers of Florida residents come. Again, migration patterns among homeless women appear to be very similar to state-wide trends.

Regardless of geographic origins, the women in our study (like Rena) tend to be long-term residents of their current area. We asked, "How long have you lived in this area?" (Interviewer instructions specified that "this area" meant the Miami, Jacksonville, Tampa, or Orlando area, as appropriate.) There was a substantial group of recent arrivals: 36 percent of the women had been in their area for a year or less (about 21% had been there for a couple of months or less). Another 12 percent of the women had been in their area for one to five years; 10 percent for five to ten years; and 42 percent, the largest group, for more than 10 years or "all of my life." Taking "all my life" to imply ten or more years of residence, the median duration area residence for the sample is almost exactly six years. But the distribution is strongly bimodal, with one large group of "lifers" and another large group of relatively recent arrivals.

Qualitative data gathered by our research group on other homeless populations in the Orlando area provide useful context for the survey data on geographic origins of Florida's homeless women. In all our samples, we find that most homeless people, although born elsewhere, are long-term residents of the state, having lived in Florida usually for an average of ten or more years. Hence, the large group of recent arrivals among the state-wide sample of homeless women makes this group somewhat distinctive. Reasons homeless people give for moving to Florida in the first place are diverse: some come to reconnect with a long-lost family member; some come planning to stay with a relative; some come for the temperate weather; many come to seek employment or get a fresh start; and some, particularly the younger, single men, are drifters who just seem to end up there after a period of wandering from place to place.

By far, the largest share of people who come to Florida and end up homeless do not arrive in the state as homeless people or as people who expect to become homeless. They leave behind homes, families, and communities and come to Florida with high hopes, eager expectations, and, usually, some sort of housing arrangement (even if this is nothing more than an understanding that they will be allowed to stay with a family member for a few weeks, while they find employment and a permanent place to live). Yet, after a period of time, these people become homeless, usually as the result of unexpected, adverse, and traumatic life events from which they prove unable to recover for some reason.

Commonly reported adverse life events that lead to homelessness include: moving to Florida with no safety net or even a definite plan in place, hoping to find employment that never materializes; loss of personal identification, often through theft, which in turn makes it impossible to secure a job, housing, or access to social services; sudden death of, or severe financial reversal suffered by, a loved one on whom the now-homeless person depended for housing or financial support; loss of a job; arrest or other law enforcement action, such as a driver's license suspension; and disabling injuries. For the women, of course, the list of homelessness-inducing traumatic life events also includes abandonment by male partners, intimate partner violence, and related relationship difficulties.

For many, the downward drift into homelessness is facilitated by alcohol or drug abuse, or the effects of being impaired by major mental illness, factors discussed in later chapters. But these prove to be less common precipitating factors for homelessness than one might guess. The modal pathway to homelessness in Florida is that people—individuals or families—come to the state because they hear that "Disney is hiring" or that jobs are easy to find in Florida. Typically, they use up most of their resources getting there or shortly after they arrive; they also discover that, while jobs are indeed plentiful, the cost of living is very high, and jobs with wages that allow one to rent apartments in Florida are few and far between. Unable to get back to wherever they came from, for a while they sleep in their vehicles, camp out in public places, or "crash"—in the vernacular—with acquaintances, friends, or relatives. Some, particularly the men, can be overwhelmed by the stress and turn violent or simply abandon their partners to homelessness. Sooner or later, all grudgingly acknowledge the reality of their situation and turn up at facilities for homeless people seeking services and assistance, whereupon they effectively become homeless.

As we see later, elements of this drift into homelessness are reflected in various ways in the hundreds of life stories of the women in our sample. Rena speaks for many in a comment quoted earlier: "It's been alcohol and drugs, or my financial situation with my job, and well, you know, one thing after another." "You know, one thing after another" pretty much says it all!

Religion and Spirituality. We are unaccustomed to thinking about the role of religion in the lives of homeless people, both men and women, perhaps because we assume (stereotypically) that their corporeal lives are too materially degraded for them to sustain a spiritual existence. But this is inaccurate: homeless people, like other people, may believe in God or a higher power, may pray for sustenance and relief, and may attend religious services. Rena confessed that she did not attend church as often as she felt she should. Of the women in our sample, about 30 percent attend religious services every week or "nearly every week"; only a quarter never attend such services. Median attendance for the sample is "about once a month" (interestingly, Rena's average). Thirty-six percent described themselves as "very spiritual," and another 42 percent said "somewhat spiritual." Only one in twenty said they were not spiritual at all.

Much the same picture emerges from the question on religious backgrounds. A mere 8 percent disavowed all religiosity by saying they had no religious background, or by describing themselves as atheists or agnostics. As would be expected in a southern state like Florida, most described themselves as Protestants (60%) or as evangelical or nondenominational Christians (10%). One in five was Catholic; one in a hundred Jewish; and the remaining 1 percent were "other" (Muslim, Buddhist, Wiccan, or Yoruba).

People who have volunteered in homeless facilities know that religiosity is ever present. Starting the evening meal without a blessing is unthinkable in these facilities. Most are visited regularly by ministers, preachers, and other religious leaders who lead evening or Sunday services, say mass, or show up in vans to take believers to church. Much of the food in these facilities is provided through faith-based volunteer efforts. Indeed, it is hard to conceive of a homeless facility that has not profited from the many biblical admonitions to feed the hungry, house the homeless, and clothe the naked. Nationwide, it has been estimated that about three-quarters of the total efforts on behalf of homeless people comes via the private sector (instead of the government), and that is principally although not exclusively from religious institutions.

FAMILIES OF ORIGIN: HARDSHIP, VIOLENCE, AND NEGLECT

In the 1990s, one of us (Wright) was involved in a research demonstration project funded by the National Institute of Alcohol Abuse and Alcoholism, called the New Orleans Homeless Substance Abusers Project (NOHSAP; Wright, Devine, and Eddington 1993). It was designed to provide alcohol- and drug-treatment services to homeless addicts in New Orleans, in order to help them achieve four main goals: sobriety, employment, stable hous- ing, and what we called "family reintegration," or the repair of broken fa- milial relationships and the reinstatement of the homeless addict as a member in good standing of his or her family.

The base-line interview for the project contained large sections that asked about families of origin: demographic composition; economic well- being; presence of fathers; interpersonal violence; alcohol and drug use among parents, siblings, and other kin; major mental illness; child neglect and abuse; and so on. An analysis of these data quickly revealed that the families of origin of the men and women in our study were themselves so profoundly dysfunctional that in most cases, "family reintegration" would have been a huge step backward (Wright and Devine 1993). Similar results were found in Hagan and McCarthy's study of street youth (1997).

Here, too, Rena's case is typical. Abused as an infant by her drug-addicted father and nearly killed by her mother, Rena spent most of her childhood and adolescence with her grandparents. Her occasional encounters with her father were almost always abusive; her mother evidently dropped out of the picture when Rena was relatively young. Abuse, abandonment, and fos- ter care placement (in Florida, more than half the foster care placements are with family members like grandparents, aunts and uncles, and older siblings) characterize Rena's early family life.

The same is true for most of the homeless women in our sample. Our questions for them began by asking them to "think back to the earliest part of your life that you can remember when you were a very young child. Who did you live with at that time?" Slightly fewer than half (49%) reported liv- ing with both their biological parents. One in four lived with their mothers; one in twenty were already living in foster or adoptive arrangements; and the remainder were living with fathers only, stepparents, or—most often, like Rena—with other relatives (aunts, grandmothers, cousins). Just 71 per- cent of the sample reported that their biological parents were married to each other at some time, and of these couples, half were divorced. When we asked the women if they had grown up in households with intact mother- father couples who were legally married and stayed married throughout the women's early lives (so-called Ozzie and Harriet households), only one woman in six or seven said yes.

The origin families of the women in the sample commonly displayed dysfunctional characteristics. The adults in the family yelled at one another in 63 percent of the cases and hit one another in 40 percent. When asked, "Did you ever leave your childhood home because of violence or abuse?" 29 percent of the women responded yes.

What sort of childhood "violence or abuse" are we dealing with here? Another question sequence asked, "When you were a child, did any parent, stepparent, guardian, or other [adult] person" do any of the abusive and violent things shown in table 2.1. Granted, some of these acts are minor. What child, for example, has not been humiliated or embarrassed by his or her parents at some time? But most of the acts we asked about are seriously abusive. And the childhood experiences of our sample with these parentally perpetrated acts of abuse are disturbingly common.

Table 2.1

Childhood experiences with neglect, violence, and abuse among Florida's homeless women

	Percent responding yes
When you were a child, did any parent, stepparent, guardian, or other adult person:	
Spank you?	68
Insult you?	53
Humiliate or embarrass you?	53
Swear at you?	52
Threaten to hit you?	52
Push, shove, or grab you?	46
Hit you with an object?	44
Slap your face?	40
Throw something at you that could hurt?	35
Pull your hair?	32
Kick or hit you with a fist?	28
Neglect you?	27
Beat you up?	27
Threaten to kill you?	19
Choke you?	17
Lock you in a closet or tie you up?	14
Threaten you with a knife or gun?	12
Burn or scald you on purpose?	8
Use a knife or gun on you?	7
Cut you?	5

Note: Responses are listed in rank-order of frequency of mention, not in the order presented to respondents in the questions (N = 737).

Being spanked tops the list, with 68 percent of the women indicating that they had been spanked. Four other acts were experienced by at least half the sample: being insulted, being humiliated or embarrassed, being sworn at, and threatened with being hit. Being pushed, shoved, or grabbed were reported by 46 percent; being hit with an object of some sort by 44 percent; being slapped in the face by 40 percent. More seriously abusive acts reported by at least a quarter of the women include being kicked or hit with a fist, being neglected, and being beat up. About one in five reported that her parents had threatened to kill her; about the same number reported being choked; and more than one in ten had been threatened with a knife or gun.

Summing up the twenty acts shown in the table, about one respondent in six reported that none of these things had happened to her as a child, and another one in six reported only one or two of the less serious acts. Charitably, then, we might conclude that about a third of our sample of homeless women grew up in home situations no more abusive than the average American home. But across the entire sample, the mean number of acts experienced was 6.4, and one respondent in ten had experienced 15 or more of the acts.

It would be misleading to describe the early childhood experiences of our sample as a universal vale of tears. At least some of the women were raised in normal homes by intact, nonabusive, nonneglectful husband-wife couples. That important point acknowledged, it is also safe to conclude that the large majority of these women were raised in generally unpleasant home environments; that many were raised in neglectful and abusive environments; and that some suffered home environments that can best be described as gruesome.

Then there is the matter of early sexual abuse, about which Rena spoke volumes and about which we have a great deal more to say in later chapters. For now, suffice it to note that Rena's rape history is by no means atypical: 51 percent of the homeless women in the sample had been "made to have sex by using force or threatening to use force" (i.e., vaginally raped) at least once in their lives, and of those who said that applied to them (N = 371), two thirds (67%) said this had happened to them at or before the age of eighteen. (Rena, recall, was in third grade when she was first raped.) In addition, nearly one in four (22%) of the women had been orally raped at least once, and of these (N = 162), 55 percent said this had happened at or before the age of eighteen. (Rena's first oral rape was when she was fourteen.) And 12 percent of the sample reported an anal rape (31% of them at or before the age of eighteen), 15 percent had someone "put fingers or objects in your vagina or anus against your will" (67% of those assaults occurring at or before the age of eighteen), and 23 percent reported one or more unsuccessful attempts at vaginal rape (48% of them at or before the age of eighteen).

Thus, while unwanted sex was by no means universal among this sample, either as adults or as children, neither could it be described as rare. One in three of these women had been vaginally raped, one in ten orally raped, and one in twenty-five anally raped by the age of eighteen. Since many women had more than one of these experiences, the percentages do not nicely cumulate, but clearly, one would not miss the mark by far in concluding that nearly half of homeless women have had forced and unwanted childhood sexual experiences. Certainly Rena did, and so did many of the other participants in our qualitative study.

These early family dysfunctions did not go unrecognized by the women. When asked to characterize their childhoods, one in five (19%) called them "very happy" and another one in four (26%) said "happy." But 30 percent could only muster a "so-so" judgment, and the remainder were unhappy or very unhappy as children. Unsurprisingly, there is a strong linear correlation ($r = .595$) between self-reported childhood unhappiness and the number of violent and abusive acts that these women reported experiencing in childhood. Very few of the women who were raped as girls reported happy childhoods, either.

Rena left her grandparents' home for a short, abusive marriage when she was eighteen. For the average woman in our sample, childhood ended either at age 19.8, the average age when they had their first child; or at age 23.6, the mean response to the question, "How old were you when you first started living on your own—you know, working for a living, paying your own bills, things like that?" (Note, then, that on average, our women had been mothers for just under four years before they started living on their own.) On average, these women experienced their first episode of homelessness at age thirty-three, and at the time of our study, their average age was 37.5 years. The four- or five-year interval between the first onset of homelessness and the present comprises the homeless histories of the sample, a topic to which we return in the concluding section of this chapter and again in the next chapter. But first we need to consider some common precipitating factors for the homelessness of many of these women—namely, their behavioral health status.

ALCOHOL, DRUGS, AND MENTAL ILLNESS

Given the life histories just summarized, it would be remarkable indeed if Florida's homeless women were psychologically well-adjusted, happy with the way their lives had unfolded, and wholly resistant to the temptations of alcohol and drugs. Study after study, of course, has confirmed that rates of addiction and mental illness are disproportionately high in all homeless subgroups: women and men, young and old, black and white. And the same is true to some degree of the homeless women in our sample.

Alcohol and Drugs. Chronic alcohol abuse is routinely found to be widespread among homeless men and women, although the reported rates vary across studies depending on the definition of "chronic abuse," sample makeup, time frame, and local particulars. Half of homeless men and one-third to two-fifths of homeless women are found to drink to excess, with some evidence that alcohol (and drug) abuse among homeless women has accelerated in recent years (North, Eyrich, Pollio, and Spitznagel 2004). Excessive drinking and drugging can also be an adaptation to the conditions of homelessness. It has been widely known for at least two decades that "in whatever setting homeless adults are studied, alcoholism is the most frequent single disorder diagnosed" (Institute of Medicine Committee on Health Care for Homeless People 1988, 60). Numerous studies also confirm a high rate of abuse of drugs other than alcohol, although again, precise estimates vary widely—from a low of 10 percent to a high of over two-thirds. Substance abuse can thus be both a cause and a consequence of homelessness; it is a risk factor that puts people on the streets, and a coping mechanism once they get there.

Despite many decades of research and thousands of published studies, there are still no agreed-upon definitions of substance abuse, misuse, or addiction, terms that tend to be used indiscriminately and interchangeably in the literature. Here we rely mainly on two self-report indicators: "Do you think of yourself as a person that has a serious [drinking or drug] problem?" and "Have you ever been treated for [alcohol or drug] problems?" The alcohol questions were not asked of respondents who said they had not had any alcohol in the previous twelve months; the drug questions were likewise skipped for those who had not used illegal drugs in the previous year. It is well known that alcohol and drug consumption is underreported in sample surveys (see, e.g., Duffy and Waterto 2006), and there is no reason to suppose this is not also a problem in our data.

Given results reported in previous studies, the homeless women in our sample use drugs and alcohol less frequently than would be expected. Only 11 percent said that the statement "I drink too much" was somewhat or very true of them, and more than half (56%) said that they had not had even a single drink of alcohol in the past year. Of those who were asked this series of questions (N = 318), 82 percent did not think of themselves as "a person who has a serious drinking problem," and 18 percent did. The latter group is 8 percent of the total sample. Likewise, of those who had consumed any alcohol in the previous year, 78 percent said they had never been treated for alcoholism, and 22 percent said they had been, the latter comprising 10 percent of the total sample.

Clearly, our results suggest less alcohol use and abuse among these women than most other studies have shown. On the other hand, these self-reports are almost certainly biased downward, and our questions were asked only of current alcohol users; questions about lifetime use and abuse, although not asked in our study, would surely produce larger numbers. In any case, taking the data at face value, only about one respondent in ten admits to an active, current alcohol problem—or, as Rena put it, "drinks like hell."

Much the same is true of drugs other than alcohol. More than seven in ten of our respondents (72%) disavow any illicit drug use in the previous year; among the remainder (N = 203), 59 percent deny that they have a serious drug problem, and 41 percent admit to one. Overall, the self-confessed problem drug users comprise 11 percent of the total sample; a slightly higher percentage (13%) admits to having been treated for drug problems. Here, too, one must assume that questions about lifetime abuse would produce higher numbers.

There is substantial overlap between alcohol and other drug problems. Among those who used both alcohol and illegal drugs at least once in the previous year (N = 142), 56 percent deny having a serious problem with either, 6 percent admit to an alcohol but not a drug problem, 16 percent say they have a drug but not an alcohol problem, and 23 percent admit to both.

Of those admitting either problem (N = 63), just over half (51%) admit to both.

Mental Illness. Clinically significant psychiatric disease is reliably reported in at least a third of homeless women (see, e.g., Silver and Panares 2000 for a detailed summary). In studies where gender comparisons are possible, rates of mental illness are always substantially higher among homeless women than among homeless men. Mentally ill homeless women have higher rates of alcohol and drug problems, have less adequate family and social support, and experience much higher victimization rates than homeless women without mental illness.

Here, too, the literature is rife with measurement difficulties, and again there are no widely-agreed-upon self-report measures available. Many of the questions routinely asked in psychiatric epidemiology surveys are absurd as indicators of mental illness in the context of homelessness—for instance, "I did not feel like eating; my appetite was poor" and "I thought my life had been a failure" (both of which are from the widely used Center for Epidemiologic Studies Depression Scale). Other empirical examples include: "Do you feel unhappy about the way your life is going?" "Do you feel discouraged and worried about your future?" "Do you feel so tired and worn out that you cannot enjoy anything?" Nearly every sane homeless person would have to answer yes to all of these questions—not because of mental disorders, but because of the material conditions of their existence (Wright, Rubin, and Devine 1998).

Lacking any obvious alternative, we again rely on the respondents' self-reports: whether they had ever "been admitted to a hospital for any psychological or emotional problems," had ever "been treated for any psychological or emotional problems as an outpatient in a clinic," had ever been told by a "health professional, counselor, social worker or other clinician" that they "had a psychological or emotional problem" or that they were "mentally ill," and whether they had ever tried to kill themselves.

The results were highly consistent across questions and, unlike our results for substance abuse, also consistent with previous literature. Thirty-six percent of the total sample reported a psychiatric diagnosis by a mental health professional; 32 percent had been admitted to a psychiatric hospital, many of them numerous times (among those ever admitted [N = 225], the mean number of admittances was 3.8); and 39 percent had been treated as an outpatient for emotional problems (among those ever treated [N = 268], the mean number of treatments was 8.6, a number seriously inflated by the 90 women in the study who reported 20 or more episodes of outpatient treatment). As if to drive home the seriousness of these women's psychiatric difficulties, 29 percent had attempted suicide at least once (15 percent more than once).

Clearly, Rena's behavioral health problems are not atypical of the women in our study, many of whom, like her, have been in and out of psychiatric treatment and rehab, and have made multiple suicide attempts. To the list of woes, we might also add physical health problems (41% of the women have "chronic medical problems that interfere with your life"), multiple incarcerations for offenses large and small (45% of the women have spent time in prison or jail), troubled family relationships (37% reported "serious conflicts" with their families in the thirty days prior to coming to the shelter), and weak or nonexistent social support networks (34% have no close friends, and 21% have just one).

It is important to emphasize that Rena and the many other homeless women in like condition and circumstance are not the muttering bag ladies or floridly psychotic basket cases in the popular stereotype of mentally ill homeless women. Most of these women, even those with significant psychiatric diagnoses, are functioning, albeit under extremely trying circumstances; contributing to their own support and well-being as best they can, given local economic circumstances; and actively involved in efforts to resolve their housing and other issues. Carey-Webb writes: "the homeless [men and women alike] range from exhausted, troubled and dispossessed people deserving of our sympathy and care to intelligent, socially aware, self-critical agents asserting and fighting for their rights and dignity" (1992, 697). Or as Amanda, one of the mentally ill women in Hirsch's *Songs from the Alley* (1989) put it so eloquently: "We are human beings, with pride, with feelings, with dignity. We all share a common problem. We are all HOME-LESS! All we want is a room with four walls, two windows, a floor, a ceiling, a door with a lock on it, and a key that fits that lock. THIS IS ALL WE WANT!"

HOMELESS HISTORIES

Homelessness is not a single condition but a vast assortment of misfortunes that culminate in not having an acceptable place to live. Every homeless person comes to homelessness via a different path, experiences homelessness in a different way, and exits the condition of being homeless through a different door. For many, as we discuss more fully in the next chapter, homelessness is a once-in-a-lifetime, transitory event; for others, homelessness becomes a chronic condition, a way of life. And there are many varieties of homeless experience between these two extremes.

Culhane and associates (1994, 1997, and 1999; Kuhn and Culhane 1998) have drawn an important set of distinctions between transitionally, episodically, and chronically homeless persons that we discuss in detail in the following chapter. For now, suffice it to say, first, that there are many fewer chronically homeless people, and many more transitionally home-less people, than is typically assumed; and second, that this is as true of the women in our study as any other sample of homeless people.

This important point is illustrated by a brief consideration of the question, "How many homeless people are there?" Obviously, the answer to this question will vary by method of counting and by one's definition of home-less.[1] But the consensus within the research community is that there are roughly a million homeless Americans on any given evening—about one in three hundred U.S. residents are homeless.

However, since some people who are homeless tonight will not be home-less tomorrow night, and vice versa, the number of people homeless on a typical night must be smaller, and perhaps far smaller, than the number destined to be homeless at least once in a typical year. The annual preva-lence has been shown to be between three and six times larger than the nightly incidence of homelessness, so in the span of a year, the number destined to suffer at least one episode of homelessness must be on the order of five or six million—call it one in fifty Americans.

And by the same logic, the number of persons destined to be homeless at least once in a lifetime must surely exceed the number who are homeless on a given night or in a given year. Survey estimates of lifetime prevalence report findings of between 7 percent and 12 percent—call it one in ten.

Clearly, if all homeless people were chronically homeless people, then the nighttime, annual, and lifetime homeless percentages would all be about the same, but of course they are not—not among the homeless in

1. One might think that being homeless is an obvious condition, but this is not so. Even the federal government uses different definitions, with that of the Department of Housing and Urban Development varying in important and significant ways from that used by the Depart-ment of Education to determine eligibility for homeless educational services. For instance, the latter includes families who are doubled up in a residence with others; the former excludes this population.

general, and certainly not among the homeless women studied here. Indeed, half the women in the sample were experiencing their first episode of homelessness when we interviewed them, and most of those women had been homeless for less than two months. As we discuss more fully later, transitionally and episodically homeless women, not the chronically homeless, predominate in our sample.

The important point revealed by these numbers is that there are vastly more people who are formerly homeless than who are currently homeless: one in ten Americans, say, versus one in three hundred. Hopper (2003) has pointed out the obvious implication: the system of homeless shelter and assistance obviously works for the large majority of homeless people. Most homeless people, in short, get over being homeless, starkly in contrast to the stereotype. Why isn't this hopeful fact better known? Hopper observers: "once people manage to escape from the streets and shelters, they typically prefer to pick up their new lives as 'neighbors,' 'workers' and 'citizens'— and not as tagged specimens of the 'formerly homeless'"; thus, "the evidence of successfully resolved homelessness—although all around us—is bound to be difficult to detect" (2003, 184). Undetected, it is not cited as evidence of the value of our collective investment in the programs that serve today's homeless people.

Just as there is no one type of homeless person, so there is no one cause that results in people being homeless, and this also is as true of our sample of homeless women as it is of any other homeless sample. One open-ended question we asked early in the survey was, "What led you to become homeless this most recent time?" While one might anticipate (or perhaps, hope for) a few obvious and common themes (alcohol and drugs, domestic violence, job loss, and perhaps a few others), the responses described a vast panoply of the toils and troubles of the human condition, an array of infirmities and misfortunes that are simply impossible to summarize:

"I became too old to pick oranges and so I was looking for someone to care for me, but I always looked in the wrong places."
"The apartment did not pass the Section 8 inspection so the landlord threw us out."
"A mentally abusive roommate."
"I was living in a small apartment with my aunt but she could not fit her son, daughter and me in."
"Bad budgeting caused us to be evicted."

"Because I was with a man who hit me and my one-year-old for six months.
     We got out and went to a shelter for battered women and children."
"I just lost control of my alcohol and drug usage."
"Because of my daughter's drug use and her mental abusiveness towards me."
"The building was condemned and I had to leave with the rest of the tenants."
"My boyfriend went to jail and I couldn't afford the rent."
"I lost my job and my husband was killed in an accident."
"I could not support myself and three children with one income and no welfare."
"My emotions were running wild. I tried to commit suicide and spent a month
     in a mental health facility."
"I wanted to relocate to Orlando to find a better job."
"I was being stalked by my husband and thought I could hide out in the home-
     less shelter."
"I was staying with a friend from the church but when he tried to force me to
     have intercourse for staying in the house, I left."

These are just a few of the responses that we pulled off the first few pages of output. Elsewhere in a very long list are car wrecks that made it impossible to commute to work, problems with immigration papers, job cutbacks, reduced hours, drug addiction, physical altercations, sexual assaults, male abandonment, divorce, domestic violence, eviction for nonpayment of rent, eviction for violating Section 8 (the federal program of housing vouchers that subsidizes housing costs for low-income families) and public-housing rules, foreclosures and condemnations of property, various family problems, deaths of caregivers, various physical ailments, even "stranded in Florida while working for the circus." As was equally obvious in the qualitative data, people become homeless for thousands of different reasons and experience homelessness in thousands of different ways.

We started this chapter quoting Rena, who said: "I'm not gonna say it's sad." But homelessness *is* a sad condition of human existence, and it is a sad reality that homelessness continues in our society. The different ways homelessness comes about for the women in this study, and the effects of those ways on the women's experiences with violence, are the topics of the next chapter.

⚌ 3 ⚌

Homelessness and Its Consequences

Just tell people never, ever let this happen to them. You have choices,
but a lot of people don't know. I mean, if anytime you even suspect that it's
gonna happen or it happens one time, get help. Just get help. Don't let the
stories continue. Do not let—don't take the "It's never gonna happen again,
I'm sorry"—it don't work. It don't work. Once they hit they're gonna keep
hitting. Once the drugs start, it's gonna continue. Just make better decisions
than some of us have made because it's not worth it and you'll end up either
dead or being homeless, or whatever. It's just not a good road to take.
There are people out there—there are a lot of places to help . . . get
the help . . . It's not worth it. It's just not worth it. —*Diane*

As we discussed in the previous chapter, homelessness is a heterogeneous
set of experiences and material conditions, not a monolithic event in life
that every victim goes through in the same way (Burt, Aron, and Lee 2001,
chap. 6; Wright, Rubin, and Devine 1998). We look now at the different
types of homelessness.

Homeless Histories

As noted, Culhane and associates (1994, 1997, and 1999; Kuhn and Culhane 1998) have distinguished between transitionally, episodically, and
chronically homeless people. The transitionally homeless are those who
experience some calamitous incident, such as job loss, fire, eviction, divorce, abandonment, or some other transitory misfortune. These people,
by definition, are homeless for only a short time before they transition back
into a stable housing situation, perhaps never to be homeless again. Remarkably, in studies where this group of homeless people can be identified,

they account for the substantial majority (more than three-quarters) of the homeless population.

The episodically homeless consist of people who, like Rena, move in and out of homelessness, typically with each episode lasting only a short time. (You will recall that Rena has been homeless on and off since she was six-teen, with around six or seven episodes of homelessness). These people have recurring episodes of shelter use that vary in length. The episodically homeless represent about a tenth of the total in Culhane and associates' studies.

Last are the chronically homeless, people who become homeless and stay in that condition for extended periods of times, often years or even de-cades. They are likely to use the shelters as long-term housing rather than emergency shelter. The chronically homeless comprise roughly a tenth of Kuhn and Culhane's (1998) samples, yet they consumed about half of the total shelter days. They tend to be older, nonwhite, and—consistent with the u.s. Department of Housing and Urban Development's definition of "chronically homeless"—they suffer high rates of mental illness and sub-stance abuse. (According to that definition, two years of continuous home-lessness is sufficient to establish chronicity.)

Interestingly, a bare majority of women in our study, 52 percent, were experiencing their first episode of homelessness when we intercepted them to participate in our study. Only time will tell if this first experience with homelessness is a unique and transitory event, the first in a series of home-less episodes, or the start of a chronically homeless existence. (Panel data would be necessary to answer this critical question.) The remaining 48 per-cent of the women had been homeless on previous occasions, 17 percent of them four or more times (with a maximum of thirty times). For almost two-thirds of our sample (64%), the longest period of homelessness ever expe-rienced was less than a year; only 9 percent had ever been homeless for longer than two years. Indeed, the time spent homeless over the lifetime (cumulated across all homeless episodes) was less than twelve months for 63 percent of the women and more than three years for only 19 percent, with a median across all participants of 0.51 years. Thus, in the substantial majority of cases, these women were relatively new to homelessness and perhaps only transitionally homeless; very few would qualify as long-term or chronically homeless women, consistent with the findings of Culhane and associates.

To begin to understand the complexity of their lives, we sought to determine the women's living circumstances in the month or so before their current episode of homeless ("the month . . . before you came to this shelter"). The most common sleeping arrangement was in "someone's apartment or house" —crashing with a friend, relative, or acquaintance. In the literature, this population of near-homeless people has come to be known as the "couch homeless," "sofa-surfers," "couch-hoppers," the "doubled up," or the "precariously housed." There are no national or even local estimates of the size of this shadow homeless population, but the regularity with which this sleeping arrangement is reported among all samples of recently homeless people implies that they are numerous indeed (Hagan and McCarthy 1997). In our sample, 42 percent reported crashing at someone's home or apartment as at least one of the ways they had been living in the previous thirty days. Other notably common responses included sleeping in their own place (31%), sleeping in a hotel or motel (30%), sleeping "on the street or some other outdoor place" (22%), living in an emergency homeless shelter other than the one where they were interviewed (22%), sleeping at a parent's place (14%), and sleeping in their cars (12%)—the only options among eighteen offered that were mentioned by more than 10 percent of the women.

It is worth noting that almost all the women we interviewed mentioned multiple living and sleeping arrangements in the prior month—a few nights in a cheap motel, a few more nights on a friend's sofa, a few nights literally on the streets, etc. This underscores the disordered and chaotic lives that homeless people lead and is an observation true of all homeless populations—male and female, young and old, black and white (Burt, Aron, and Lee 2001).

Contrary to what might be expected, only about one in six of these women (16%) was living alone just prior to their current homeless episode. One in three was living with a spouse (32%), a dependent child (31%), or both. As indicated above, some were living with parents (21%) or other relatives besides children (11%), and a few were living with friends (9%). Regardless of the circumstances just prior to the current episode, at the time they were interviewed, 53 percent said they were homeless "by myself," 12 percent were homeless with another adult (but no children), 24 percent were homeless with their children (but no other adult), and 11 percent were homeless with both children and another adult (i.e., an intact husband-wife household with children—the number who indicated that their adult partner was not a spouse or "intimate partner" was vanishingly small). Most of those who were homeless with an adult partner (about a quarter of the total) had been with that partner for more than a year (71%; N = 168); thus, most of these adult partnerships predated the onset of homelessness (as opposed to meeting men and partnering with them while homeless).

So how did these women end up in a homeless shelter? We asked them what they thought had led them to become homeless this most recent time. Consistent with the apparently transitional nature of their homelessness, the most consistent responses had something to do with the lack of money. Many women noted that a job loss, either their own or that of a partner, resulted in an inability to pay their bills, including rent. Resulting eviction notices either put them on the street or led them to the shelter. For some women, the sheer force of circumstances prevented them from keeping jobs and therefore caused them to lose the ability to pay their bills. Consider the woman whose work hours were first cut and who was then transferred to a different work location. Lacking the means to get to the new location, she was unable to keep her job. Although she was living with her mother at the time and could presumably have continued to do so, she felt guilty about not being able to pay her share of the household finances, so she left her mother's residence.

Sometimes, financial challenges intersected with experiences of violence. One woman responding to an open-ended survey question told us that she had lost her employment and as a result was unable to pay her bills. Not long after that, her boyfriend became violent, and she was forced to leave her home. Another common pathway to homelessness was living arrangements that did not work out. Many women noted that before they were homeless, they were living with relatives; however, alcohol or drug use, overcrowded housing, or lack of finances often forced them to leave, either on their own or because family members asked them to. One woman in our quantitative survey had just gotten out of jail; not being familiar with the area, she was unable to find employment and consequently could not keep up with her bills.

Some women were unable to pinpoint a specific event that led them into homelessness. Natalie, for example, recalled the following:

> My sister was here in Orlando; she was diagnosed with terminal cancer. I had
> become disabled, was not able to work anymore and I had started drawing on

disability and she needed somebody to stay with her because she was going through testing and chemotherapy and that kind of thing. So I came here to be with her and she passed away last year. Last June. And I don't know, it was just something that happened to me. I just got so lost so long that I didn't feel like I belonged nowhere, didn't have nobody, didn't know what to do.

For many of these women, moving out of homelessness will prove difficult, as four in ten of them do not have a phone number where they can be reached, or a valid driver's license. Prospective employers will therefore find it impossible to follow up after any job interviews, and they may find their potential employee unable to get to and from the job or limited in the type of work she is able to do. These challenges have not gone unnoticed by the women in our study. One-third stated they believed their homelessness had affected their ability to get or keep a job. Women commented that the lack of a stable residence was one of the main issues they faced, along with not being able to dress properly for job interviews, not having an address, and difficulties staying clean. This vicious cycle only gets worse for women the more often they find themselves homeless.

The Impact of Homelessness

How does time without a home influence physical and mental health, options for survival, and strategies for staying safe? These topics have been widely researched, and the available literature is extensive. An early but still telling review is that of Dennis, Levine, and Osher (1991). In a wide-ranging review of studies then available, the authors found it obvious that "homelessness places people at greater risk for specific health problems and also complicates treatment . . . Individuals with chronic physical or severe mental illnesses are more vulnerable than others to homelessness" (815). The finding of higher levels of both physical and mental illness among homeless people has since become a research commonplace.

The distinctions among chronically, episodically, and transitionally homeless people require more differentiated conclusions, however. Transitionally homeless people are generally homeless for shorter periods of time, homeless less often, much more likely to be homeless for strictly economic reasons, subject to fewer behavioral health issues, and therefore generally healthier than episodically or chronically homeless people. In contrast, the

U.S. Department of Housing and Urban Development definition of "chronically" homeless people includes being homeless by reason of substance abuse, mental illness, or physical disability, so by this definition, all chronically homeless people have illnesses of this general sort.

HEALTH ISSUES

In general, there is scarcely any aspect of a homeless existence that does not compromise physical health, or at least greatly complicate the delivery of adequate health services. Life without adequate shelter is extremely detrimental to physical and mental well-being. Minor health problems that most people would relieve with something from the home medicine cabinet become much more serious for people with no access to a medicine cabinet and no money to purchase palliatives. Ailments that are routinely cured with a day or two at home in bed can become major health problems if one has neither home nor bed. Much that ails people requires little more than tender loving care, but tenderness, love, and care are often in short supply within the context of homelessness.

The major features of a homeless existence that impact directly on physical well-being are an uncertain and often inadequate diet and sleeping location, limited or nonexistent facilities for daily hygiene, exposure to the elements, direct and constant exposure to the social environment of the streets, communal sleeping and bathing facilities (for those fortunate enough to avail themselves of shelter), unwillingness or inability to follow medical regimens or to seek health care, extended periods spent on one's feet, an absence of family ties or other social-support networks to draw upon in times of illness, extreme poverty (and the consequent lack of access to health care), and a host of related factors (Institute of Medicine Committee on Health Care for Homeless People 1988; Wright and Weber 1987). Shelters for homeless men, women, and children may well present optimal conditions for the transmission of infectious and communicable diseases. Likewise, street environments are often unsanitary and therefore infectious. Widespread physical and sexual abuse is a further complication and risk factor.

A vast amount of literature has documented health issues related to the status of being homeless, and they clearly affected the women in our study (Brickner et al. 1990; Wright and Weber 1987). A significant proportion of the women told us they were experiencing some type of health problem at the time of the interview. For many, chronic health conditions played a major role in their everyday existence. Health conditions such as asthma and high blood pressure were commonly mentioned, followed by diabetes and depression. Although chronic health problems have been identified as a significant issue for homeless populations in general (Hwang 2001), when we considered how different characteristics of women's homeless experiences were associated with these health conditions, only age at the first instance of homeless was significant. Women who reported a chronic health condition were first homeless at an older age than women who did not report such a condition. Exorbitant medical bills can lead to an inability to pay rent and can therefore be a pathway to homelessness; here, it can be mentioned that about half of all personal bankruptcies that occur in the United States are the result of burdensome medical bills (Kvall 2008). More than one-third of the women in our study said that they were taking prescribed medication on a regular basis for a medical problem.

Living with chronic health issues requires some level of contact with the medical system. Are homeless women able to gain access to medical personnel? Almost all of the women in our study had gone to a doctor within the past year. At first glance, this figure seems high; however, the women at the Jacksonville shelter were all given a medical assessment when they entered the facility; the Tampa shelter has a pediatric clinic for children and makes referrals for adults; and the Miami and Orlando shelters both partner with local Health Care for the Homeless clinics to provide primary care. Thus, the high percentage of respondents recently seen by a doctor is a result of proactive policies in place at the participating shelters, not a statement about the general accessibility of the health care system to homeless people.

Keisha may be more representative of the homeless women who face difficulties when they need healthcare. Unable to work steadily due to heart problems, Keisha had five different jobs in one year. Consequently, she did not have health insurance; when she experienced chest pains, she went to the emergency room because she had nowhere else to go. Overutilization of emergency room services among homeless persons is widely reported (e.g., Smith et al. 2000) and is a leading hidden cost associated with homelessness in virtually all u.s. cities.

We asked respondents where they went to get medical or dental care when either they or their children needed it. Although almost half of the women reported that they received medical care from a doctor's office, just over 20 percent receive their care from a free clinic, and just under 10 percent go to an emergency room for medical care. Women who receive their medical care from somewhere other than a doctor's office may be less able to establish any type of continuity of care. Further, it is likely that their medical visits are for crises rather than regular checkups or preventive medicine. Approximately one in ten of the women indicated that they could not afford medical care, perhaps one reason to delay care or to wait until the only option is to go to an emergency room.

In addition to objective questions about health, we asked the women to subjectively assess their health. The "subjective health status" question we employed was identical to the health question asked in the General Social Surveys (GSS). As the following table indicates, while slightly more than 60 percent of our sample indicated that their health was good to excellent, the corresponding percentage for the United States as a whole is higher (76%). So homeless women are more likely to be in fair or poor health than the overall population, hardly a surprising result. Of note, however, is that variations in homeless experiences were associated with health self-assessments. Both the number of times homeless and the total time homeless were negatively associated with self-perceived health status. The age a woman was first homeless was also negatively associated with self-perceived health status.

In addition to physical health, homelessness also impacts mental health and well-being. Women who experienced a greater number of homeless episodes had significantly lower levels of self-esteem than women who had been homeless fewer times. Moreover, women who were first homeless at a younger age had lower self-esteem. Clearly, the very fact of being homeless has a significant impact on the level at which these women value themselves. For more on this and related issues, see chapter 9.

Table 3.1

Homeless women's assessment of their health (percent)

	Florida four-city study	*United States (GSS)*
Health excellent	21.8	32.0
Health good	40.4	44.0
Health fair	28.8	19.0
Health poor	8.8	6.0

RISKY BEHAVIOR

We know from the literature that being homeless is potentially dangerous, and that homeless individuals may engage in risky behaviors as part of their survival strategies (Hagan and McCarthy 1997). The women in our study illustrate these processes. Just over 10 percent of the women in the quantitative portion of our study had worked as prostitutes, and 13 percent had worked as exotic dancers. Although the number of women in our study who reported involvement in some type of sex work was not large, their chances of involvement significantly increased if they had been homeless more often and had first become homeless at a younger age. For younger women, perhaps with only limited education and with no family support, sex work may be one of the few ways in which they can earn enough money to survive. For some of the women, involvement in sex work seemed to happen almost by chance. Consider Tracy's matter-of-fact account of her entry into prostitution:

Tracy: Yeah. So I went home and my momma said either you go to school, or you go back where you were. So I went back to school. It lasted a year. I was in ROTC, everything. I was very intelligent. Very intelligent. And I didn't want to hang no more. So I took off. At the age of 15, she told me you need to get on the bus and go to Philadelphia and get some help.

Interviewer: What was in Philadelphia?

Tracy: Rehab centers. Things like that. The little town I grew up in didn't have nothing like that. So she gave me bus fare to get to Philly. I got to Philly and ran into some pimps, man. I ended up in DC.

Interviewer: Is that where—?

Tracy: I got turned out at. I started whoring.

Interviewer: When you went out there and you met—how did you meet—?

Tracy: What happened was there was a limousine that had the name of a band that I know—I can't ever remember right now. It was a limo and they were like, want to go to DC with us? I thought they were a band, but they were working for the group. And they were like, you want to go and I'm like yeah, why not. And they had a bus and I jumped on the bus, and went to DC. Got to DC, he talked shit, he said well, I got me another wife, but I don't need neither one of you. So I went on the bus with the clothes on that I got there with, took off, started walking. A black church picked me up and let me stay

> in their room for a while. I left there and went down to the bus station and
> ran into a real pimp. I stayed with him for five years.

Tracy had left her home and, in a city where she had no contacts, hooked up
with a pimp, beginning a career in prostitution that lasted twenty-seven
years. Even now, she prostitutes herself when she needs cash.

In subsequent chapters, we speak at length about the experiences with
violence that these women have had—while they were children, as adults
but before the onset of homelessness, and once they became homeless.
Indicative of the perceived risks of life on the streets, 55 percent of the
women said they were "very concerned" about their personal safety, and
one in five made a point of carrying something with which to defend herself against street predation. Nearly two in three (64%) said "yes" to the
question whether they considered themselves to be a victim of violence,
nearly half (43%) had changed residences at least once to escape violence or
avoid a violent situation, and slightly more than one in four said that "violence or abuse committed against you by an adult partner in your last residence" was either the main (14%) or at least one (12%) reason why they
were currently homeless.

We began the previous chapter with Rena's story, and it is appropriate to
return to her in this chapter. When asked, "As a woman do you feel more
vulnerable being homeless?" Rena responded: "Well, a woman is more at
risk than a male if she's living out there on the streets without shelter, of
course. Oh, my God, yeah." She went on:

> Yes, because of the rapes, which can happen with a female or a male, but more
> so with a female because she's alone out there. There's just a bunch of sick men
> out there who don't care what they do to a person. Or they have no control over
> themselves when they rape a person. There's a lot of rapists and child molesters
> out there, running around this environment, right now, today. And I just feel that
> a female is more vulnerable when she's on the street by herself. I mean, she
> might decide to go and have a beer or something with some guy, or some guy
> might take her to his house. And she may just give in to this guy because she
> feels like, hell, she's already homeless and so you know, "What have I got to
> lose?" Well, you have a lot to lose. It's called self-respect.

Ronald Reagan once said in an interview about the homeless, "well, you
know, most of these people are, well, we might say, homeless by choice"

(Roberts 1988). He attempted to justify the remark with reference to the large proportion of homeless people who, like Rena and many others, struggle with mental illness, addiction, and other personal problems; whose educations are suboptimal; and whose participation in the labor force is spotty. But for women like Rena and the over 700 others whose troubled lives and souls supply the data for this book, how can this possibly be a realistic analysis of how they ended up homeless? Listen to Rena one more time:

> Look, I got a problem. I need some help. Hell, I'm crying out for help. You think I want to drink? You think I want to come here . . . ? Hell no! But I want to thank these people . . . for letting me come here and giving me a chance. You think I don't want to do that? Of course I do. Of course I do . . . I have some issues and situations and things I need to deal with. I know I do. So help me. Don't kick me out. *Help* me out, because I really want to help myself.

Perhaps what remarks about choice in this context truly underscore is the limited number and appalling nature of the options available for those who ultimately become homeless.

= 4 =

Homeless Victims and Perpetrators of Violence

> He kept hitting me, pinching me, and I just refused to say anything.
> But when we were about a mile from the house, he reached over and
> backhanded me. And when he did, I don't know what made me do it,
> but I did the same thing to him. As soon as we got to the house . . .
> he picked me up by the throat, slammed me up against the
> refrigerator—it felt like he had broke every bone in my body
> and I was just hanging there, shaking. —*Natalie*

The early research on violence against women was crucial to raising awareness that millions of women were victims of violence, often at the hands of
a partner or spouse (see, e.g., Straus, Gelles, and Steinmetz 1980; Straus
and Gelles 1990). From that point forward, scholars sought to increase
public awareness of this type of violence as a significant social problem. At
the same time, researchers worked to refine the tools used for the measurement of this often hidden violence, the types of violence that intimate partners use, and the typical motives behind violence between intimate partners. As a result of this increased scholarly and public recognition and
methodological advancements, a considerable amount of research aimed at
more fully understanding the dynamics of violence has emerged.

Today, national surveys of the violence that women have experienced
include a new understanding that violence varies among different groups
or populations, because members of certain groups have different access to
social resources (e.g., income, healthcare, available transportation) and
different types of structural barriers (e.g., education, employment, stable
housing) than members of other groups. Homeless women are one population for which the evidence about violence is still being collected. As the

National Research Council said over a decade ago: "Differences among sub-groups in the causes of violence against women could have important im-plications for prevention and intervention strategies. Subgroups about which information is lacking include racial and ethnic minorities, lesbians, migrant workers, immigrants, *the homeless*, the disabled, and the elderly" (1996, 90; emphasis added); research since then has done relatively little to address this gap.

As indicated in chapter 1, although there is general agreement that rates of violence against homeless women are high, studies vary on their assess-ment of just how high and how consistent these rates are. These differences are most likely a result of researchers' using a variety of measures to assess the types and frequencies of violence that homeless women experience, varying samples of homeless populations across the country, and different sets of questions about the experience of violence.

In this chapter, we remain broad in our focus, comparing our study re-sults with national rates of violence against women and locating this violence within a context of gender inequality. We then discuss a range of gender differences among homeless women and homeless men in terms of victim-ization and perpetration. Later chapters will probe in more depth particular aspects of violence and homelessness in the lives of the women in our study. This section, then, provides a backdrop for subsequent discussion.

Studies of Victimization

Our survey of homeless women in four Florida cities yields estimates on the amounts and types of violence these women have lived through. And although a comparison of our sample of homeless women with a national sample of women in general is not an ideal comparison, it is at least a start-ing point. A more appropriate comparison would be with a national sample of homeless women, but we know of no such sample. Furthermore, since we used the same measures of victimization as were used in the National Violence Against Women Survey (NVAWS; Tjaden and Thoennes 2000), a comparison between our results and those of that national study is a logical first step. Keeping in mind that all women are at much higher risk than men of sexual assault, rape, and intimate partner violence, comparisons reveal that the women in our study were much more likely to be victimized than the women in the NVAWS. For example, while the national survey shows that slightly over 50 percent of women in general experience any type of violence during their lifetime, our study shows that approximately 80 percent of homeless women experience violence. Compared to women in general, homeless women tend to experience much higher levels of sexual assault: approximately 18 percent of the NVAWS sample indicated that they had been the victim of a completed or attempted rape, whereas in our sample, 56 percent had been the victim of a completed or attempted rape. This is more than triple the percentage of women in the national sample.

Homeless women also experience other types of violence at higher rates than the women in the NVAWS. Indeed, while slightly over 50 percent of the national sample had been physically assaulted (e.g., had something thrown at them or been pushed, grabbed, shoved, slapped, hit, kicked, bitten, shocked, beaten up, threatened with a weapon, or had a weapon used against them), nearly three-quarters (75%) of the homeless women had been victimized in these ways. Also, the three-quarters of the women in our sample who had been physically victimized had experienced many of the specific types of physical assault three to four times more often than the women in the national sample who had been victimized. Finally, one-quarter (25%) of Florida homeless women had been stalked, while 8 percent of the women in the NVAWS had been stalked.

We find the same type of difference between the amount of violence Florida homeless women face at the hands of an intimate partner and that faced by women in the NVAWS. Specifically, 45 percent of the women in our sample who were raped reported this crime (either attempted or completed) at the hands of an intimate partner, and 79 percent were stalked at least once by an intimate partner. The rate of reported stalking by an intimate partner was more than four times higher among the homeless Florida women than among women across the United States. Of the women in our study who were physically assaulted as adults, fully 88 percent were assaulted at least once by an intimate partner. This was almost three times greater than the percentage of women in the national sample who reported at least one assault.

Gender and Violence

We can locate understandings of violence against women within contexts of inequality and the corresponding construction of ideologies, social norms, and attitudes. Barnett, Miller-Perrin, and Perrin (2005) note that although events like the 1994 O. J. Simpson trial have brought violence against women more to the forefront of public consciousness, on a personal level, acceptance of such violence remains at surprisingly high levels. There is little social tolerance for female victims, who are often blamed for not leaving abusers in spite of the many factors that keep women in violent relationships (Worden and Carlson 2005) and the risks of victimization when they try to leave (DeKeseredy and Schwartz 2009). Patriarchal beliefs play a role, including justifying the use of violence to reinforce male dominance, privilege, and power, and the subjugation of women. Eigenberg notes that "patriarchal social structures effectively use violence against women as an important means of social control" (2001, 1)—i.e., violence or the threat of violence keep women "in their place." Research about women's victimization finds that it "occurs within a wider context composed of responses from social agencies and general beliefs and attitudes about the relationships between men and women, husbands and wives, and about the use of violence to achieve various aims" (Dobash and Dobash 1998, 9).

Within this framework, women who follow traditionally established roles and who are viewed as appropriate victims are more likely to receive public support and sympathy (Meyers 1997). They are treated as "good girls" (Madriz 1997) and less often held responsible for their own victimization. Homeless women are subject to an even more complex ideology because their status as victims is embedded in the larger context of perceptions of homeless individuals in general. A highly stigmatized and socially excluded population, the homeless are seen as an unwanted segment of society (Brinegar 2003) with little social utility or worth (Miller and Keys 2001; Seltser and Miller 1993; Snow and Anderson 1993). Often, their identity as homeless persons puts them in one of two overly simplistic categories: victims of circumstance, or personally responsible for their situation (Donley 2008). This dichotomy calls to mind Kathleen Ferraro's (2006) critique of the "angel" or "demon" labels ascribed to the incarcerated women she interviewed. As children, the women in our study were more easily perceived as innocent victims of terrible violence, but as homeless adults, they are commonly viewed as unruly women and thus seen as less deserving of public sympathy (Ferraro 2006). Because of their stigmatized status, homeless individuals are also at risk of hate crimes. Nearly 500 violent hate-crime attacks against the homeless were documented in the period from 1999 to 2005, for example (National Coalition for the Homeless 2009).

In her book about woman battering, Eigenberg demonstrates "how society minimizes violence by intimates in favor of definitions of crime that concentrate on violent crime committed by strangers" (2001, 1). She further argues that social definitions of crime and the public policies that follow from them would probably be extremely different if the magnitude and seriousness of intimate partner violence were addressed. Indeed, a major aspect of the social context of violence against women relates to its normalization as an act, and trivialization as a crime. For example, criminal justice and legal systems have historically been reluctant to become involved in what is perceived as a "private" family matter (Felson and Ackerman 2001). Barnett, Miller-Perrin, and Perrin (2005) find from a synthesis of investigations that police arrest about one-fourth of batterers, prosecutors decide to prosecute about a third of those arrested, and about 1 percent of those prosecuted receive jail time beyond that served at arrest. The perpetrators of intimate partner violence receive considerably shorter sentences than perpetrators of other crimes; more than half do not even arrive at the confinement stage. An analysis of 2,670 cases of domestic violence revealed a court dismissal rate of 51 percent (Belknap et al. 1999). Shelters, which can provide emergency care and safety to the victims of intimate partner violence, are embarrassingly underfunded by federal and state governments and turn away approximately 32 percent of applicants because of lack of resources (U.S. Conference of Mayors 1998). Studies conducted by the U.S. Department of Justice note that victims of violence against women have difficulty obtaining services at every level of the criminal justice system (Hofford and Harrell 1993), and that this reflects historical precedents and patriarchal beliefs that are entrenched in this system (Feder 1998; Parker 1997).

Though women are much more frequently victims of violence in the home (Dobash and Dobash 1992; Hollander 2001), a gendered analysis of fear finds that, overall, women feel most vulnerable to violence—ranging from objectification and harassment to assault and attack—in outdoor, public spaces (Gardner 1995). This "shadow of sexual assault" (Kenneth Ferraro 1995) contributes to women's geography of fear (Valentine 1992), or how women negotiate interpretations of risk and safety on a daily basis. The gendered nature of fear also means that women and men tend to view safety very differently. For women, safety encompasses both sexual and physical aspects, whereas men think of safety purely in physical terms (Stanko 1990, 1993). Homeless women, however, are rarely able to manage gendered fears of sexual violence by escaping the public or communal environments that trigger them. In fact, we found that fears of sexual victimization are reinforced by daily experiences that expose homeless women to violence.

Overall, our study shows that homeless women were significantly more concerned with their personal safety than were homeless men, as is true for women and men in general. For men, safety concerns centered on attacks by strangers, and the potential for fights as well as health concerns related to staying in the homeless shelter. Men who had been homeless for longer periods of time were significantly more concerned about their personal safety. In contrast, women were primarily fearful of sexual assaults. Again, for homeless women, being in public spaces is typically unavoidable and consequently heightens their feelings of vulnerability. Central to this fear is the possibility of sexual assault. The majority of women in our study said that the fear of being raped was their single most important safety concern. Their homeless status exacerbated this fear, certainly for the large number of them who stated that their biggest personal safety concern was walking the streets at night and being afraid that someone would attack or rape them. Other women stated they were fearful of the other residents at the homeless shelter. This fear was not unfounded, as 14 percent of the women who reported victimizations ranging from assault to theft told us that the victimization happened while they were staying at a homeless shelter. Still others believed the shelter afforded them some protection from the dangers existing just outside the door. This was literally the case for one of the qualitative participants, Sherie, who watched a man attack a woman directly outside the homeless shelter where she was staying:

> I've seen a man beat a woman in the bushes over there by the [shelter] one night . . . When the ambulance got here, she was unconscious. And somebody just happened to hear her little, tiny scream. And looked over in the bushes, there [the man] was. I've seen so much in the past couple of years that I don't take a chance on going to the 7-Eleven by myself at night. I don't go by myself as a rule in the daylight. I don't go wandering around by myself.

Women also expressed a fear of being found by their abusive partners. In response to an open-ended survey question, one woman said she was most concerned that her abuser would return and "finish what he said he would finish." Another woman said her involvement in a number of abusive relationships led her to fear getting close to people in general. The combination of generalized fear and specific instances of victimization resulted in a sense of despair so deep for some women that they could not think about the future beyond the next day. In fact, a startling number of women said they were afraid they would not live another day.

Although personal safety concerns seemed to center on physical and sexual violence, the violence and victimization experienced by the women in our study were often embedded in a context of power and control, and it is from within this context that violence or threats of it carry even more weight. Seeing this as a web of abuse (Kirkwood 1993), we begin to understand the extent to which the women we interviewed were trapped between abusive partners and surviving on the street. Regardless of any physical or sexual victimization experienced by the women in our study, the dynamics of power and control illustrate the types of relationships they were caught in. In a sequence of questions asking about characteristics of the woman's adult intimate partner, for instance, just under half (46%) of the women reported that their partners experienced jealousy and possessiveness often or always. Our study also found that victim isolation was common, with just over a quarter (28%) of the women stating that their partner limited their contact with family and friends often or almost always. Further, 42 percent of the women in the quantitative part of the study reported that their partners often or always insisted on knowing where they were, and who they were with at all times. By monitoring women's activities, abusers were able to exact punishment and maintain control over their partners (Johnson 2008). Notably, these adult experiences for the women dovetailed with the abuse they had experienced as children and reinforced already existing feelings of degradation, exacerbated by name calling, public humiliation, and put-downs (see chapter 6). As a result, some women reported a pervasive sense of inadequacy in addition to a fear of their abusers. About one-third of the women said that the only way to make the abuse stop was to go into hiding in an attempt to escape their partner. Some of these women hid in the homeless shelter. Unlike most domestic violence shelters, whose locations are usually kept secret, homeless shelters are public places—everyone knows where they are. Consequently women's fear of being found by their abusive partners may be justified.

As we have demonstrated, ideological attitudes feed into the prevalence of intimate partner violence against women, while at the same time making it difficult for victims to get the attention and services they need. Social norms and beliefs thus have real consequences and are part of the social context in which violence against women occurs. The women in this study, whose homelessness intersected with intimate partner violence in different ways, have unique experiences rooted in this social context. We continue by discussing gender differences among the homeless in terms of victimization by, and perpetration of, violence.

Gender Differences in Victimization

One of the problems in the existing literature is a general absence of comparison groups. Therefore, an important strength of this study is our ability to make comparisons between homeless women and men. For this purpose, a somewhat modified questionnaire was developed and administered to roughly 100 men who sought shelter at The Men's Pavilion in Orlando. This facility is on the same site as the Center for Women and Families, where our Orlando women were recruited, and both facilities are managed by the Coalition for the Homeless of Central Florida. Although the men in our study were residing in the same facility as the women, their backgrounds and histories in many cases were very different from those of the women.

Detailed analyses of gender differences in background characteristics and homeless histories revealed that:

- The men are predominantly African American (75%), whereas the women are much more diverse.
- Women, on average, had more children than men.
- A greater proportion of women than men reported that they were divorced, widowed, or cohabiting; men were more likely to be married.
- Women, on average, had a greater number of marriages than men.
- Although both men and women first became homeless in their early thirties, men were homeless an average of one and a half years longer than women, were homeless more often than women, and had longer episodes of homelessness.
- A much higher proportion of men were homeless by themselves. In con-

trast, women were likely to be homeless with children, an adult partner, or both.

• Although men experience higher overall rates of victimization, women were more likely than men to have left their childhood home due to violence or abuse.

Above, we established that actual rates of victimization among homeless women in our study were significantly greater than those of women in general. Here we consider the patterns of victimization among homeless women compared to homeless men. Even though women fear violent victimization more than men, men are more likely to be victims of violence than women (Catalano 2006). We investigate here first whether the same is true for homeless people, and second whether the patterns of victimization are gen-

Table 4.1

Gender differences in the experience of violence: Lifetime victimization

Type of victimization	Women (N = 737)	Men (N = 91)
Total rape	**55.9**	**NA**
Completed	53.9	14.3
Attempted only	22.9	NA
Total other assault	**72.2**	**86.8**
Threw something	46.0	54.9
Pushed, grabbed, shoved	62.0	65.9
Pulled hair	35.3	7.7
Slapped, hit	58.4	50.5
Kicked, bit	27.8	30.8
Choked, tried to drown	34.5	11.0
Hit with object	32.5	49.5
Beat up	45.2	48.4
Threatened with a gun	20.1	46.2
Threatened with a knife	24.9	37.4
Used gun	7.4	29.7
Used knife	14.3	36.3
Rape and/or physical assault	77.7	90.1
Stalking	25.4	3.3
Total rape and other assaults	78.3	90.1

Note: Numbers are percents. NA = not available.

dered—and if so, how. Consider first the information in table 4.1, which illustrates different lifetime victimization types, regardless of victim-offender relationship, for homeless women and men in this study.

As expected, men were more likely to report any lifetime victimization than women. However, there are important gender differences in the patterns of victimization. Men's victimization, regardless of their relationship with the perpetrator, is driven primarily by physical assault, whereas a significant proportion of women were likely to be sexually assaulted or stalked. Similar findings regarding sexual assault were found by researchers using data from the NSHAPC (Lee and Schreck 2005) and RAND's Course of Homelessness Study (Wenzel, Koegel, and Gelberg 2000). Gender differences in concern for personal safety reflect actual victimization experiences in this way. Within the category of physical assault, there are also important gender differences. Women, for example, were more likely to report having their hair pulled or being choked. In comparison, men were more than three times as likely to report having a gun used against them, and just over two times as likely to report a knife attack. Consistent with the different type of victimizations experienced by men and women, women were much more likely to be victimized by an intimate partner (see table 4.2). When all offenders are considered, women are less likely than men to be physically assaulted in their lifetime; however, when only intimate partner offenders are considered, women are more likely than men to be physically attacked. These numbers provide further support for the relationship between violence against women and homelessness.

Gender differences also emerge when we consider other types of victimization more commonly associated with street crime. For example, men were much more likely than women to have had items stolen from them;

Table 4.2
Gender differences in intimate partner victimization

Type of victimization	Women (N = 737)	Men (N = 91)
Rape (both attempted and completed)	25.1	NA
Physical assault	63.0	39.6
Stalking	19.8	0.01

Note: Numbers are percents. NA = not available.

men were also three times more likely to have been stabbed, and more than six times more likely to have been shot at. In contrast, there were no gender differences in experiences of being pickpocketed. Is homelessness related to these victimization experiences? Lee and Schreck argue that the marginality of homeless persons may be the primary explanatory factor for their victimization: marginality "underscores the importance of structural forces (an affordable housing shortage, economic and policy changes, etc.) that push some poor people over the threshold of shelter security, leaving them without the protection from crime offered by a dwelling unit or residential neighborhood" (2005, 1074). For our shelter sample, the answer is yes and no. Almost a quarter of the men were victimized while staying at a homeless shelter, more than the 14 percent reported by women. For both men and women, having their personal items (such as shoes or wallets) stolen while at a homeless shelter was the most commonly noted type of victimization. No men mentioned any type of sexual victimization taking place at a shelter, whereas several women recalled instances where they had been groped or fondled.

The perception of being a victim is also gendered. In this study, women were more likely than men to see themselves as victims of violence, with about a quarter of the men and two-thirds of the women considering themselves a victim of violence. Do these gender differences remain when asked about the impact of such violence? More than a third of the women stated that being a victim of violence had interfered with their ability to get or keep a job, and just over a quarter said violence had interfered with their ability to find housing. By comparison, 24 percent of the men said that their victimization had interfered with their ability to get or keep a job, and 12 percent that it had interfered with their ability to find housing. Clearly the impact of violent victimization is felt more severely by women than men. Since the women were significantly more likely than the men to be victimized by an intimate partner, it follows that it is more typically this type of violence that interfered with their housing and employment. This finding reinforces reports on the causes of homelessness, which have consistently noted that violence against women is one of the factors related to homelessness (U.S. Conference of Mayors 2008), and that a significant proportion of the victims of violence report homelessness as one of the consequences of the violence they experience (Kershner 2003).

Gender Differences in Perpetration

In addition to differences in the types of victimization experienced by men and women in our sample, we also considered differences in offenses perpetrated. Our results are consistent with other research on homeless populations. In Wright, Rubin, and Devine's (1998) New Orleans study of homeless alcohol and drug abusers, for example, illegal activities produced the largest share of abusers' incomes. These activities included petty crime, theft, drug dealing, and—for the women—prostitution. Indeed, researchers have shown that homeless women employ survival strategies such as prostitution in order to trade sex for money, shelter, or drugs. Of course, these types of activities put women in potentially dangerous circumstances and increase their risk for victimization. In our study, only a small proportion of the women indicated that they had worked as prostitutes or as strippers. About half of the women who had been prostitutes were still prostitutes at the time we interviewed them. We also found that while only about 2.5 percent of the women in our study were currently working as strippers, 11 percent had worked as strippers at some point. What is perhaps more disconcerting, however, is that about a fifth of the women who had worked as prostitutes and 7 percent of the women who had worked as strippers said that they had been forced to do so.

In our study, additional reports of criminal offenses were common, but there were some notable gender differences. Similar to other homeless populations studied (see, e.g., DeLisi 2000; Fischer, Ross, and Breakey 1993), the women in our sample had committed different types of criminal and violent acts. The two most frequently reported criminal offenses were shoplifting and drug possession. Almost a third of the women indicated that they had shoplifted as an adult and almost 20 percent reported having possessed drugs. Still, men were much more likely than women to be involved in drug offenses such as possession and sales. Far fewer women than men indicated that they had committed such offenses as vandalism, selling drugs, and forgery, or violent crimes such as weapons offenses, armed robbery, and assault.

Indeed, table 4.3 reveals that men were four times more likely to report that they had perpetrated domestic violence than women (33% compared to 8%). Since Western gender roles, socialization patterns, and institutions such as schools and churches strongly discourage women from using violence, any report of this kind of perpetration "must be viewed as emerging from more intricate motivations" than those of men (Dasgupta 2001, 4). A pathways perspective recognizes that "girls' crimes are usually grounded heavily in the social conditions of their lives and their roles as females within a patriarchal society" (Gaarder and Belknap 2002, 485). For example, patriarchy includes notions of women's sexual objectification and commodification, which are manifest both in girls' self-concepts and in their oppression (Bartky 1990; Bordo 1993; Chapkis 1986; Griffin 1981; E. Martin 1992). These social constructions affect the ways that girls and women may be treated and devalued, as well as the coping and survival strategies they utilize. In their analysis of two qualitative studies of delinquent girls on the street, Miller and White (2004) find that girls had to negotiate gendered power imbalances and stereotypes of weakness and sexual availability. Offensive violence was a counteractive measure, a practical choice made while "taking into account the gendered nature of their environments" (186). Any examination of women's violence, then, must consider that girls and women have uniquely gendered lived experiences.

The marginalization and desperation that accompany women's homelessness intersect with the gender frame of women's violence in this study. Economic instability, social exclusion, physical risk, victimization by intimate partner, and fear of sexual attack are some of the realities we have identified thus far, and we will illustrate more. Preoccupation with daily survival, feeling beaten down, and inability to access opportunities to improve life circumstances solidified a context of "cumulative victimization" (Wesely 2006, 2009) for the women in this study. They learned that they lived in a dangerous world, and if they did not protect themselves, no one else would. This is illustrated by some of the qualitative findings, such as the case of Mo, who has a long history of victimization and perpetration of violence that began in childhood. Punched, kicked, and beaten by her father as a child, Mo tried to tell authorities about the abuse but was ignored. She says: "since I was a little kid, [my dad] always said, like, I fell down or something." She recalls years of wearing long pants, turtlenecks, and "always sweating but scared to go to school with regular clothes on because of the bruises." As a young teen, she tried to fight back. When she did this, her father called the police, and she was charged with domestic violence. Eventually, Mo's school reported her father's abuse, and she was removed from

Table 4.3
Crimes committed by homeless men and women (percent)

	Women (N = 737)			Men (N = 91)		
	Yes	Arrested	Convicted	Yes	Arrested	Convicted
In adult lifetime, have you ever done any of the following?						
Shoplifting	27.7	15.3	9.0	56.0	35.2	27.5
Vandalism	2.8	0.8	0.3	9.9	2.2	1.1
Drug possession	18.0	10.2	6.9	53.8	47.3	42.9
Drug selling	6.5	2.8	2.6	30.8	67.9	22.0
Public intoxication	10.6	4.1	2.6	19.8	14.3	7.7
Loitering	6.6	1.9	1.2	18.7	15.4	11.0
Disorderly conduct	7.7	4.9	2.8	15.4	13.2	8.8
Forgery	6.2	4.6	3.9	9.9	8.8	6.6
Weapons offenses	2.8	2.4	1.5	14.3	76.9	11.0
Burglary, larceny	2.0	1.5	0.9	13.2	12.1	9.9
Robbery, armed robbery	2.3	1.8	1.2	13.2	90.9	11.0
Assault	7.9	6.2	3.3	27.5	25.3	16.5
Homicide, manslaughter	.08	0.5	0.4	0	0	0
Driving while drunk	8.7	4.6	4.5	23.1	15.4	14.3
Contempt of court	5.3	3.3	2.8	19.8	18.7	14.3
Child abuse or neglect	4.7	1.8	0.7	1.1	1.1	0
Domestic violence	8.1	6.1	2.8	33.0	31.9	23.1

her home by child protective services, which contacted her mother. Mo re-calls: "They made her come get me, and I lived with her for a couple of years. But after so many years of taking all my dad's crap, when I got there, I started beating the shit out of her." Mo's mother, a drug addict, is cur-rently in prison for first-degree murder. Mo also violently attacked her step-mother: "And we were fighting, and I guess after so many years of dealing with so much crap I snapped and took it out on her. So I stabbed her . . . I stabbed her repeatedly in the head, neck, arm, and then I bit a hunk out of her arm. I was really—I had a lot of pent-up anger." Mo served jail time for this attack. For Mo, violence became a strategy of coping and resisting cu-mulative victimizations and abuses. Although she was incarcerated, little was done to address the underlying context of her violence.

Mo's references to her victimization as years of "taking crap" and having "pent-up anger" point to an underlying theme in many of the women's statements. "Violent resistance" as a type of intimate partner violence is almost entirely perpetrated by women (Johnson 2001, 2008), and both in-cludes and extends the meanings of self-defense. Although some of the women interviewed in our study did respond immediately and violently to attack, violent resistance is not always limited to such sequences of provo-cation and response. Women considered perpetrating violence as a realistic strategy when they recalled past abuses and anticipated future victimiza-tion. In addition to child abuse, Mo was also victimized by a number of boyfriends in adulthood. The father of her son tried to kill her while she was pregnant:

> His father beat me up every day for about six and a half months. Choking
> me . . . He said, "If you tell anyone, I'll kill you and the baby." And the last time
> was when he set me on fire real bad. Both my eyes swelled up. My nose was
> like—it was almost to the side. My mouth—my lips were so big from being
> steadily hit. I had handprints around my neck. I had handprints on my arms
> from him grabbing me. And you could see the marks on my stomach from
> where he had been kicking me.

When asked if that was the most recent abusive relationship she had experienced, Mo responded: "I've been in other relationships, but I tell the guys who I date, I say, if I think you're gonna get physical—the moment I think you're gonna get physical or any type of violence toward me, I'll hurt you first before you can hurt me." Hayley, who had been seriously injured in three different relationships, had a similar attitude: "because I'm built tough . . . I'll beat the shit out of a man if he fuckin' ever tries to touch me."

This zero-tolerance attitude translated into a refusal to be passive during violent attacks. April recalled a particular beating by her boyfriend that occurred as he tried to remove their newborn child: "I put him through a sliding glass door. I picked up a big, heavy office style chair that we had in our apartment and threw it at him and he went through the door. Because he was trying to beat me and take my child from me, and I just came home from the hospital with her. So that ain't working." Other women interviewed in our study perpetrated violence in adult relationships where there was very little threat of violence from a particular partner, although previous partners had been extremely violent—a telling resistance to cumulative violence. Junie told us how she reacted to a partner who was not violent: "He was always telling me you're gonna have to stop slapping me. I don't like that. And I realized—and he understood because of what I went through and he was like, you know, you're just always fighting and that's not the way. And he changed me."

As is typical with most crimes and offenders, only a small proportion of the women who committed crimes were arrested and then convicted of illegal activities. Still, it is notable that nearly half of the women in our sample had spent some time in prison or jail at some point in their adult lives, as had almost the entire sample of the men. These numbers are much higher than for the general u.s. population: according to the Department of Justice, the lifetime chances of someone's going to state or federal prison are 11.3 percent for men and 1.8 percent for women (Bonczar 2003). Our numbers are more consistent with (but still higher than) data from the nshapc (Burt, Aron, and Lee 2001), in which over two-thirds of the men and approximately one-third of the women had been in jail, state or federal prison, and/or a juvenile detention center for more than five days.

Of the women in our study who had committed acts of violence against their intimate partner, 6 percent were arrested, and almost 3 percent of them were convicted for that offense. Additionally, five percent of the women were on probation, parole, or community control at the time of their interview. Consistent with greater levels of self-reported perpetration of criminal offenses, men were more likely than women to report currently being supervised by the criminal justice system.

Particularly relevant for our sample is the link between victimization and incarceration. More than half of the women in jail in the United States are victims of physical or sexual abuse (James 2004). Kathleen Ferraro (2006) notes that official data show that about 60 percent of incarcerated women have experienced abuse, but that qualitative studies and estimates reveal even higher numbers—from 75 percent to 90 percent. In our study, experiences of childhood and adult victimization were strongly and significantly associated with having spent time in jail or prison. Further, women who left their childhood home due to violence were one and a half times more likely to have spent time in jail or prison.

> The [existing] policy focus on controlling the behavior of individuals rather than attending to deteriorating social conditions and opportunities contributes to an environment in which the experiences that lead people to commit crime are discounted. It also helps explain the dramatic increases in incarceration that have placed the United States in the position of incarcerating a greater proportion of the population than any other nation. (Ferraro 2006, 4)

For the women in our study who ended up incarcerated, that outcome was visible proof of the structural conditions of inequality and disadvantage that characterized their lives.

Conclusions

The relationships between women, homelessness, and violence are complex. This chapter has provided a broad picture, looking at and comparing rates between our study and national samples, and between homeless men and homeless women. We found that the homeless women in our study were much more likely to be victimized by intimate partner violence, rape, and stalking than women in the general u.s. population—sometimes dramatically so. Although women in general experience much higher rates of these victimizations than do men, homelessness clearly plays a role in making women even likelier targets. Victims of rape or intimate partner violence who are homeless women are met at best with social and institutional indifference; at worst, they face attitudes that hold women responsible for their victimization. Fears of sexual and physical violence were difficult to escape for the women in our study, since they rarely had a safe space to themselves, and their past experiences of violence reflected their vulnerability.

Many of the men and women who participated in our study reported extremely high rates of victimization. When we compared men and women in the sample, we found several differences. Men reported higher rates of physical victimization, whereas women reported higher rates of sexual victimization. This is consistent with general patterns of criminal victimization, in which women are much more likely to be victimized by an intimate partner. When only intimate partner offenders are considered, women are more likely than men to be physically attacked.

In addition, men reported somewhat different patterns of criminal offenses and much higher conviction rates compared to women. Men were four times more likely to report that they had perpetrated domestic violence than women. This chapter has noted that gender frames how women and men perpetrate crimes, and that the milieu from which women's violence emerges must be included in discussions of that violence. Qualitative interviews further illustrate the importance of the often ignored context of cumulative victimization. Although the design of our study does not allow us to determine the causal order of committing offenses and experiencing victimization, the argument can be made that the activities associated with criminal behavior can put individuals at an increased risk of victimization. However, beyond the gender differences in victimization and offending that mirror those in the general population, the extremely high rates of victimization among the homeless may be the most noteworthy finding of this portion of the study. Previous research as well as results from our study (see chapter 9) have suggested that victimization is associated with a number of negative consequences, and consequently homeless individuals who experience higher levels of victimization are at an even greater risk of these negative outcomes.

5

Risk Factors and Routine Activities

Because I wasn't stable as far as having an environment that I could go
home, wash up, eat and go to sleep and be safe—because men would
attack you. Anywhere. If you weren't alert and streetwise. —*Eliza*

It is apparent that many homeless women are victims of violence. At the
same time, there are a variety of circumstances leading to victimizations,
and a range of frequencies along which the victimizations fall. It is useful
to understand the environmental and individual factors that are significantly
related to the differing amounts and types of victimization experienced by
homeless women. In this chapter, we will examine the risk factors and routine activities that heightened the vulnerability of the women in our study.

Most of the previous research that focuses on women's early victimization experiences—such as childhood physical, emotional, and sexual abuse—
finds that these types of adverse experiences are some of the main explanatory factors for many of the psychological, social, and environmental troubles
adult women face. As we have discussed, when these types of abuses happen to children, they are significantly more likely to become crime victims
when they are adults (Browne 1993; Browne and Bassuk 1997; Clarke,
Pendry, and Kim 1997; Gilbert, El-Bassel, Schilling, and Friedman 1997;
Goodman 1991; Schaff and McCane 1998; Simons and Whitbeck 1991;
Wenzel, Leake, and Gelberg 2001). Recently, research examining the factors associated with women's victimization has shifted focus in order to
consider some additional variables that may be influential. This important
shift theorizes the presence of factors that help explain the clear conclusion
that criminal victimization is not distributed randomly across neighbor-

hoods, individuals, and time but instead has regular, identifiable patterns. The resulting routine activities theory considers locations containing many would-be offenders; persons or places that are valuable or have valuable items with them; and the protection available in an area, or the individual strategies people use to protect themselves—and how all these relate to criminal victimization (Cohen and Felson 1979).

Since its development, scholars have used the routine activities theory to identify lifestyles or routine behaviors that tend to increase people's risks of being victims of violence (Mustaine and Tewksbury 1997a). Typical risky behaviors include being out in public, being in or very near locations where victimless crimes occur (as perpetrators of those crimes often commit violent crimes, too), or being where many people are loitering. Other dangerous routines include bringing conspicuous valuables when going out in public; frequently going out in public without being prepared to defend yourself—e.g., being unable to put up physical resistance or to escape; being too young, physically disabled, or hampered, perhaps by the presence of young children; or being too frightened; and not having taken safety precautions—such as having a cellphone, Mace, or a whistle; bringing a dog along; and going out in a group (Miethe and Meier 1990). These types of lifestyles or regular routines increase a person's risk of criminal victimization because they bring to one location at the same time both offenders and victims, without the presence of people or devices for preventing crime. Conversely, other types of lifestyles tend to minimize individuals' risks for victimization—for example, spending leisure time at home, going to the ATM only during business hours, leaving expensive jewelry at home, minimizing the amount of cash on your person, carrying Mace, and going out only in groups of friends.

Specifically as it pertains to homeless people, previous research using routine activity theory has found lifestyles that include alcohol and drug abuse, prostitution, greater time spent on the street, greater numbers of homeless episodes, trading drugs for shelter, and panhandling are all predictive of elevated victimization risks (e.g., Alexander 1996; Bennett 1995; Geissler et al. 1995; Kilpatrick et al. 1997; Tyler, Hoyt, and Whitbeck 2000; Tyler, Hoyt, Whitbeck, and Cauce 2001; Wenzel, Leake, and Gelberg 2001; Wright, Rubin, and Devine 1998). Indeed, routine activity theory is particularly well suited to an examination of homelessness. Here again, the central propositions highlight the relationship between being homeless and being a crime victim. First, the routine activities of homeless persons create many opportunities for criminals simply because of the sheer amount of time the homeless are near potential offenders. Second, the subjective value of any particular target is likely related to the value that the target has to the potential offender—perhaps because the target may be carrying valuables, or because victimizing the target is satisfying or beneficial. Although it is unlikely that homeless people carry much of value to someone who is housed, other homeless people might find their possessions quite desirable. Additionally, crime considerations surely also include how well guarded targets are, how willing any witnesses may be to intercede, and the presence or absence of official forms of crime intervention, such as law enforcement officers in the area, or a neighborhood watch program. Homeless people cannot secure their possessions and, because their lifestyle is often illegal, are regularly forced to live in areas with lower police presence.

Homelessness Women and Routine Activities Theory

It is hard to imagine a lifestyle that does more to increase one's contacts with potential offenders in locations conducive to criminal opportunities than the lifestyle of homeless persons. Our purposes in this chapter are twofold: first, to describe in some detail the routine activities of the women in our sample; and second, to examine those activities as predictors of the amount of violence these women experience. One important aspect of the routine activities of homeless people, plausibly related to their victimization, is the daily struggle for overnight shelter. Many of the places where homeless people sleep render them easy targets for victimization. Further, as we noted in chapter 4, homeless people who spend their nights in indoor shelters are not immune from victimization: many shelters are dangerous places, where victimization is a frequent occurrence. We will now describe the lifestyles and routine activities of our sample of homeless women.

We asked the women about their customary sleeping arrangements. Some of the most common places where the women had slept recently were in a hotel or motel (42% had slept there recently), in their own apartment or house (31%), or in someone else's apartment or house (30%). Less frequently, women had recently slept on the street or in some other outdoor place (22%), at an emergency homeless shelter (22%), at a parent or guardian's apartment or house (14%), and in a car or other private vehicle (12%).

What immediately stands out is the large proportion (31%) that spent their nights in their apartments or houses. This provides some support to previous research indicating that the homeless are episodically rather than chronically homeless, as nearly one-third of the women in our sample had been housed at least once during the most recent month. Additionally, the high proportion of these women who had slept at someone else's apartment or house, or in a hotel or motel, suggests that for a good part of the time during their periods of homelessness, these women are not sleeping on the street or in another insecure, semi-public location. Although the numbers are much smaller, some homeless women in the sample had also slept in abandoned buildings, alcohol or drug treatment programs, jails, psychiatric facilities, movie theaters, cars, after-hours clubs, and crack houses.

We also asked the women to indicate their usual sleeping locations, to give us a better sense of their everyday lives. The women reported sleeping primarily either at their own place or at the home of a family member or friend. Another 15 percent of the women indicated that their usual sleeping place was a homeless shelter. Other women reported primarily sleeping in cars, outside of homes, or in parks, albeit these percentages were relatively small. Again, the large number who reported primarily sleeping in their own places or with family members and friends is a useful reminder of that fact that most homeless women (and men, for that matter) are transitionally or episodically homeless. As explained earlier, the transitionally homeless are people whose homelessness is a temporary situation, often lasting for a week or less—for example, people who are between apartments, or who have hit a rough patch in the road and need a few days or a few weeks to get back on their feet. Perhaps as many as three-quarters of the homeless fall into this category. The episodically homeless are people who bounce in and out of stable housing situations.

Of the twenty women interviewed in the qualitative study, eleven had spent at least one night on the street, as opposed to in a shelter or a friend's house, a hotel, or some other temporary lodging. Most (but not all) of the time, these eleven women were alone while on the streets. Some of the women interviewed spent extended time living on the street; others had done so less frequently, only when they had nowhere else to go. Homeless women who were on the street for longer periods included those who still held down a job and those who drifted through the day, focused on the bare necessities and survival. One example of the latter group is Marion, who frequently spent the night in airports prior to the heightened security there in response to the 9/11 terrorist attacks. After 9/11, she often slept at bus stops. She reported:

> I stayed in bus stations for two or three days at a time. Because I didn't have nowhere to go . . . I used to walk around until I got tired and then lay on the bus stop bench, lay on the sidewalk, sleep in the bushes. I slept in bushes, I slept on concrete sidewalks, I just followed the lead of other homeless people. I used to see them sleeping in front of doorways. I just go lay down and sleep with them.

Where homeless people sleep is an essential element in identifying why some homeless women are more frequent victims of crime. In addition, where they are likely to just spend time (even in the daylight hours) is related to their exposure to possible criminal offenders. Here, we find that more than four in ten women customarily spent time in places where homeless people gathered; just under a third spent at least some days and nights in places where drugs were bought or sold; and about a quarter spent some time where prostitutes solicited clients. Needless to say, being in any of these places increases the risks of victimization.

Another important activity for homeless women—indeed, for anyone— is getting sustenance. Eating, and where people do it, may or may not increase their odds of being criminally victimized. We asked our sample of homeless women where they usually ate their meals before coming to the shelter. Consistent with their reports of staying with family and friends, about a quarter of the women indicated that before coming to the shelter, they ate meals with someone they knew (e.g., a family member or friend). In addition, about a third of the women ate meals at their own homes. Relatively small proportions ate their meals at social service agencies such as soup kitchens, senior centers, or church meal programs in the period immediately before coming to the shelter. A small proportion of the women did not know where they would get their next meal. Marion's desperate circumstances again serve as an example:

> I used to go five or six days without eating, but believe it or not, after awhile your body gets used to not eating. You know, after awhile, what's hungry? You have severe hunger pains and after that you don't be hungry. You're thirsty a lot, but

you don't be hungry. I used to beg for water all the time. But you stink so bad, people don't want you in their business stinking, and they say, you know, "Do you have the money to buy it?" You don't have no money to buy it, no water.

Homeless women are not increasing their chances for being victimized by criminals by eating in such public places as shelters and soup kitchens, at garbage bins, or wherever they could find food. Theoretically, homeless women who are eating with friends and family should be safer than those homeless women who are eating out in public. But our numbers reveal that this is not the case, as women who are eating in public places are not more likely to be criminally victimized than those who are eating with friends and family. In fact, as we have already seen, women are frequently victimized by people they know. This explains the apparent theoretical contradiction: women who eat in public are not putting themselves in any more danger than those who eat with their friends and family, they are simply altering the identity of who is likely to victimize them—perhaps their husband, if they are eating with their family, instead of a stranger, if they are eating in public. Additionally, those who are victimized by husbands, boyfriends, or other family members are at the mercy of these offenders when the women come to them for shelter or food. This dependency can prolong their victimization experiences.

This is what happened to Cammie, one of our interviewees, who was homeless with her violent partner. Typically, he controlled everything, including her money and food. In the scenario Cammie describes below, she had some money and tried to buy something to eat for herself. Her partner flew into a rage, causing their eviction from the hotel where they were staying.

And then wherever we would stay, I don't care if it was a hotel or whatever, I would start trying to get a job and I was financially dependent on him. There were days I couldn't even get him to leave me a dollar twenty-five to get on the bus to go get a job . . . And we moved into the worst sections of—I mean, I didn't even know sections like that in Orlando existed. Hotels, trailers, you name it. And we happened to be in a hotel and he hadn't worked all week long. I did have a job. I was working at the time and I had gotten paid on Tuesday and I'd paid for the room through Saturday and he had done nothing but lay in the bed all week long. And I came home from work on a Thursday, I opened up the door to the room and there he was laying on the bed—you know, curtains drawn, totally dark in there—and I put my bag down and changed my shoes, and he says, "Where do you think you're going?" And I said, "I'm going to Wendy's and get something to eat." He said, "Bring me back something." I said, "If you want something to eat, get up out of that bed and walk over to Wendy's with me." And he said, "You better not come back from there with only food for yourself." And I came back in with food for myself and I started to eat it and all hell broke loose . . . he ended up throwing me across the room. He tore the rotor cuff in my shoulder . . . the next day, the manager threw us out of the room.

Mo, another interview participant, met her boyfriend while she was selling crack (she was not a user). Her life became intertwined with his almost immediately, and she soon became pregnant by him. She became homeless to be with the future father of her baby, and they stayed in an abandoned building until she was about six and a half months into her pregnancy, bathing with a water hose hooked up to the ceiling, and going to various shelters to get a free lunch or dinner. This situation finally ended when Mo was beaten badly by her boyfriend.

Another important element in the daily routines of individuals that influences their risks for victimization is how often someone is in a location where victimless crimes or other public nuisances are taking place—because persons who commit victimless crimes or perpetrate public mischief are also likely to commit crimes of violence. Therefore, we asked the women in our sample how much time they typically spent during the night in areas were homeless people gathered, where drugs were bought and sold, and/or where prostitutes were soliciting clients. Interestingly, the vast majority of the women indicated that they never spent their evenings in these types of locations (56%, 69%, and 78%, respectively). Nonetheless, a significant minority of homeless women do spend at least some of their time in these crime-ridden locations, and theoretically, these women would be more likely to be criminally victimized.

Other locations where people spend their time are important for considerations of how daily routines influence victimization risks. To assess the types of locations where the homeless women typically spent their days and evenings before coming to the shelter, we asked them an assortment of questions. We found that during a typical day, these women generally spent most of their time at crowded outdoor locations, at private indoor locations, at crowded public indoor locations, traveling from one location to another, and at work. Very few of the women were in school or spent time in outdoor locations that were not crowded. These patterns of behavior indicate that the women were quite likely to be in insecure, public locations, which theoretically increases their risk of victimization—particularly if these areas have high crime rates.

Other important elements in determining people's risk of victimization are their views about the social problems they see as plaguing their communities. We asked the homeless women about problems and general social disorganization in the places where they spent their average days and nights. We found that prior to becoming homeless, most of the women in our sample did not feel that they spent time during a typical day or evening where there were relatively serious social and community problems. In all cases, less than a third of the sample reported serious problems in any of the specific areas we asked about. This again suggests that most of the homeless women did not feel they were in places where social disorganization reigned, and where their safety may have been compromised. Nevertheless, nearly a third of the women did feel they spent at least some time in areas with such serious problems as trash and litter laying around, inconsiderate or disruptive neighbors, too much noise, people being drunk or high in public, unsupervised youth, and vacant houses and unkempt lots.

We also asked the homeless women to identify the neighborhood structures where they spent time before coming to the shelter, another element in describing their lifestyles. During their typical days, the highest proportions of women spent time in locations where there were convenience stores, grocery stores, churches, and neighborhoods made up primarily of homes (over 70% reported spending time in each). The women also spent time in these locations during the typical evening. The types of locations where the women were least likely to spend a typical day or evening were places where there was gang graffiti or gang activity, a gathering place for prostitutes, a high school, or a nightclub. Again, here we find that most of the women are not engaging in the types of lifestyles typically associated with violent victimization, but a smaller proportion are.

Similarly, we found that just under half of the homeless women spent a good deal of their typical day in locations where they encountered groups of people hanging out on the street; just over half spent their days indoors, and a much higher percentage reported spending their evenings indoors. It is likely that when the women were indoors, they were at home, work, or school. Correspondingly, when they were outdoors, they were likely to be traveling from one location to another or spending time in outdoor locations, many of which were crowded.

When asked who they spent their holidays with, the women reported that they were with children, other family members, and/or partners or spouses. A quarter of the women indicated they typically spent holidays with their family members. Another 10 percent spent holidays with their partner or spouse, and an even greater proportion (17%) spent holidays with children. At the same time, 18 percent said they typically spend holidays alone. This summary makes it plain that many or most of the homeless women in this sample do not live in isolation, with no social support networks. A significant proportion of them have more or less regular contact with family members and friends, and holidays are no exception. Theoretically, this lack of social isolation should insulate many of the homeless women from criminal victimization.

Although many of the women in the sample told us they had places to sleep and eat, this does not mean they are not part of a mobile population. In fact, about three-quarters of the women reported traveling from one location to another at least once a day, and a little over a third reported traveling at least once from one location to another in the evening. The women reported using public transportation or walking when they traveled from one location to the next during the day. None of the women reporting taking a cab to get around, and only a few reporting hitchhiking, biking, or having someone else drive them. Similar patterns are evident for travel at night, with the exception that a higher proportion of women then get from one place to another in private transportation (their own or someone else's). Most of the women, however, report using public transportation. It is in traveling to locations where they need to be—e.g., from home to work, or from a place where they can eat to a place where they can sleep—that many homeless women are in risky situations. Taking public transportation and walking are two ways of getting around that leave the homeless in greater proximity to potential offenders, in places where there are fewer guardians willing and capable of interceding.

Another part of travel that is important for considerations of safety is with whom one travels. For example, if the homeless women in our sample were alone, then their safety might very well be compromised. If they traveled with others, they might be safer—assuming that the others with whom they travel are capable of defending them. We found that when the women went about their daily business, over half of them were alone; a much smaller proportion reported being with their children. Similarly, when going about their business at night, the women traveled primarily alone or with their children. In contrast to daytime travel, a higher proportion of women traveled at night with friends and adult partners. Once again, we find the women are traveling in public locations without capable guardians. In those situations, we would expect to see their risk of victimization to be increased.

Women's Homelessness and Victimization Risks

Having described the daily routine activities of these women, we can now turn to the real strength of routine activity theory, which is the identification of and explanations for which types of daily routines are the most risky. Lifestyles that are significantly related to victimization are an important element in the experience of violence that is part of the lives of homeless women.

As noted, when assessing routine activity theory, most recent scholars have gauged not just where people spend their time, but the conditions and types of people that are present in these locations. Those factors are indicators of the degree to which someone's daily routines put him or her at risk of victimization. Further, some of the activities in which people engage can influence their suitability as targets and their ability to protect themselves. Below, we discuss the results of the analyses we conducted to assess which types of lifestyles influenced these homeless women's victimization risks. We found many aspects of the women's lifestyles were significantly related to their experiences with criminal victimization.

Assessing where people go is important because people who spend time away from home or in locations where the risks are higher are more likely to be victims of criminal violence because they are in closer proximity to potential offenders. We found that women who, prior to coming to the shelter, spent more days in locations where drugs were being bought or sold, or in places where prostitutes were soliciting clients, were more likely to be victims of violent crime (defined as sexual or physical crime and stalking).

Tamara is one participant in our qualitative research who lived on the streets for an extended period of time. She sees risks as an inherent part of life there for women:

Being a homeless woman that's on the street, that's dangerous. You have homeless men, and it's co-ed when you're sleeping on the street. It's co-ed and some
of them approach women and want women to give them favors sexually. Too,
sometimes, they get bold enough, they try to rape the women and a lot of homeless women do be raped, raped and murdered. They will murder them in alley-
ways and you will find homeless women in the dumpster. Someone slit her throat.

Indeed, the risks the women faced for violent victimization were significantly related to where they slept prior to coming to the shelter. Specifically,
women who slept at home or at the home of a family member or friend had
significantly lower risks of victimization. Women who slept in a vehicle
prior to coming to the shelter had significantly higher risks, as did women
who had slept in an indoor location other than a home (such as a flophouse),
and women who slept at a shelter prior to coming to the current shelter.
These findings are all in the expected direction, as each particular location
that is associated with higher rates of victimization would be expected to
have higher numbers of potential offenders.

Sleeping outdoors—for instance, in one's car—surely makes one a more
vulnerable target. Like flophouses, such locations provide little guardianship, limited or nonexistent familiarity with the other people there, propin-
quity to crimes such as prostitution and drug dealing, and contact with any
number of potential offenders. These locations are not inaccurately described as hot spots, and, as we have just seen, being in them increases the
risk of victimization.

Diane, like many of the homeless women in our study, moved around
from hotels to trailers to shelters in search of a place to sleep. She described
how a rented room in a house quickly turned into a high-risk situation:

We met a guy in a motel one day and this guy had mentioned that he had an
extra room he could rent out. And so one day when I was walking to work, I
seen this guy and I asked him if he still had that room and he was like, "yeah,
you can move in." It ended up being $175, $200 a month to stay there and I
thought, well, I'm working, I can afford that so I went to the Salvation Army
[shelter], packed up my stuff, just thinking, I can get out of here! I don't have
to be homeless. I can have my own place. So I went, packed up my stuff and
moved in with him. I found out later he was a crack dealer. And he started
being real possessive of me.

One night Diane witnessed this man, her "landlord," stab another man nearly to death. Shortly after, the landlord threatened to kill Diane and her children if she left the rented room. After eleven days, she escaped and went to the police. The police helped Diane find the homeless center at which we interviewed her, and the man is being charged with attempted murder. She will be testifying at his trial.

Our quantitative data revealed that sleeping in hotels or motels was one of the more common sleeping arrangements of homeless women. Victim-ization there could be at the hands of an intimate partner, like the episode described in the quote from Cammie. Other victimization was perpetrated by strangers. Molly, for instance, spent some time at the Vacation Lodge, an extended-stay hotel that she says was oriented toward people with lower incomes. During her time there, she was raped anally by two men who broke down the door to her room. Understandably, Molly felt extremely vulnerable following this attack and tried to protect herself by putting booby traps around her door. Ultimately, she ran out of money and had to leave the Vacation Lodge. With nowhere else to go, she spent one night on the street, sitting up awake at the bus stop. In the morning, on a tip from some-one she had met at the Vacation Lodge, she took the bus to the homeless shelter. For Molly, her time at the hotel was more damaging and dangerous than her one night on the street. However, she also feared for her safety while at the bus stop, in part because of her earlier experiences of sexual victimization.

Our findings also suggest that shelters are not always safe places to go when one is homeless. Certainly, shelters can and do provide respite, shelter, food, and possibly some assistance in receiving services. But they do not al-ways provide high levels of physical safety, and routine activities theory tells us why: shelters are full of potential offenders (see, e.g., the perpetration rates discussed above) and provide limited opportunities for guardianship (even shelter staff are limited in their guardianship roles by understaffing, underfunding, or preoccupation with other goals and clients). Several of the women in the qualitative portion of our study reported being harassed or threatened by men at or near the shelter. For instance, April said:

> See, at night we can leave [the shelter] but we have to be inside by nine o'clock unless we have a pass. But it gets dark earlier now. And you have to walk out that back gate to go to the store if you need to go to the store. And there's a lot

of homeless guys back there and yes, they all talk a lot of trash . . . If you show
fear, it's like a pack of wolves . . . Everybody know when you walk back there
through the pavilion back there, through that back gate, you're gonna get talked
to, somebody's gonna say something. And I don't think there's been a night
gone by that a woman's walked through that gate that [there] hasn't been something said to them.

Not surprisingly, the sleeping location that appears to be the safest is
one's own home or the home of a family member or friend. This is to be
expected, since kith and kin are more often guardians than offenders (though
they prove to be offenders often enough). The implication, however, is that
the best defense against the risks of victimization that result from being
homeless is—not to be homeless!

Regarding current lifestyle factors, women who typically spend their
evenings outdoors had higher risks for victimization. This too is consistent
with routine activity theory, as scholars typically posit that people who are
outside have higher risks of violent victimization because they are in closer
proximity to potential offenders, in locations where guardianship is compromised.

Where women spent the greater portions of their days was also significantly related to their risks for violent victimization. Specifically, women
who spent more time at work during the day were less likely to be victimized. Likewise, women who spent more of their day in a crowded indoor
public location had lower risks for victimization. These findings initially
seem to be contrary to the expectations of routine activity theory, as researchers typically find that being at work is more risky for criminal victimization than being at home (Lynch 1987; Mustaine and Tewksbury 1997b;
Wooldredge, Cullen, and Latessa 1992). This is probably because work can
be a relatively public location and certain workplaces may be occupied by
disgruntled and impatient customers (or employees, for that matter). However, given the particular nature of our sample, it may be that for homeless
women, work is a safer location in which to spend the day than the possible
alternatives (e.g., on the street). Further, even though the indoor locations
they frequent are crowded, and should therefore have more potential
offenders, it may be that the types of indoor locations where these homeless women go are safer because the outdoor locations the women frequent

are even more dangerous, with more potential criminals but also fewer potential guardians.

Also consistent with the theory's expectations, women who traveled frequently from one location to another during the day had higher risks for victimization, as did those who traveled frequently in the evening. The amount of time women spent at a private indoor location in the evening was significantly related to their risks of victimization.

To combat the well-founded fears of victimization while homeless, the women who spent a limited amount of time on the street often used the strategy of not sleeping at night. Like Molly, Ruby spent one night on the street after she ran out of money while staying at a hotel. Unlike Molly, who was alone, Ruby was with her husband. Still, she said it was "awful. Awful. I never thought a day in my life I'd be out here in this cold. It was cold . . . I didn't sleep. No, I didn't [feel safe]. I was so tired, I was so tired. But I had to sit up all night long." Rena also noted that any time she had to spend a night on the street, she did not sleep. She said: "I'd just sit up all night. Every time. Every single time. Sit straight up. That's right. Tired as hell and just sit up." She would sleep during the day, when more people were around. Tracy, another participant in our qualitative study, worked as a prostitute for twenty-seven years. She reported having 275 prostitution charges on her record, having been in sixty violent situations, and having gone to the hospital eleven times for related injuries. She has been raped, shot, and kidnapped, and she says she will never spend a night on the street:

> Hell, no. Uh-uh. Single female go sleep outside? I don't think so. Because other homeless people, you never know what they're going to do, and I take some serious meditation [sic] that knocks me out. And I walk in my sleep and shit. No, no, no, no. Ain't no way in God's creation would I sleep out there by myself. No.

Jensen and Brownfield (1986) have pointed out that the dichotomy between victims and offenders is often artificial, in that being an offender is itself a risk factor for victimization. As we saw earlier, very large numbers of the women in our sample were both victims and offenders. Are our recent offenders also likely to be victims? To address this question, we created a variable with the value of one if a woman had recently committed any of the following types of crimes: shoplifting, vandalism, drug possession, drug dealing, public drunkenness, loitering, disorderly conduct, forgery, weapons offenses, burglary or larceny, robbery, assault, homicide or manslaughter, DUI, contempt of court, child abuse or neglect, and domestic violence— and the value of zero otherwise. We then compared this variable to the variable measuring violent victimization. As anticipated, there was a significant relationship in the predicted direction: offenders are more likely than nonoffenders to be victims themselves.

An important theoretical conclusion is that routine activities theory provides a moderately successful explanation of victimization patterns in this sample of homeless women. This conclusion is important because scholars have seldom examined models built on the principles of routine activity theory within specific populations, so the relative applicability of this theory to specific groups has been largely unstudied. Additionally, these findings clearly reveal that the factors that predict the risk of victimization for homeless women encompass the three central elements of routine activity theory: exposure to offenders, target suitability, and presence or absence of capable guardians. As such, it is clear that utilizing the unique lifestyles and routines of homeless women provides a good test of the theory as well as a moderately good explanation for why some homeless women are more likely to be victims of violence than others.

Conclusions

Both the quantitative and qualitative life experiences of these homeless women illustrate the explanatory power of routine activity theory. By virtue of being homeless, these women led much more dangerous lives than housed women; in fact, the homeless women were victimized more often in a single year than most women are during their entire lives. Additionally, some of the homeless women were forced to have daily routines that placed them at even greater danger for criminal victimization than other homeless women. The types of locations where many homeless women sleep, eat, travel, and otherwise negotiate life are in communities characterized by disorganization or crisis. In these locations, crime flourishes because residents are less likely to cooperate with each other in their efforts to prevent and effectively handle the vast amount of crime, public nuisance, and disregard for one another that is present. As the women aptly noted, being homeless is stressful, scary, and generally awful. And, as has become evident, the more a homeless woman must have daily routines that place her in proximity to these types of neighborhoods, the more likely she is to be violently victimized.

= 6 =

The Childhood Nexus

In the neighborhood I grew up in, it was nothing to see a woman dragged, knocked down, stomped and beat . . . So many women, including my mother—they stood there and they took it . . . So I took on that generational trait. You were just supposed to take it. —*Eliza*

Eliza's quote above alludes to a "cycle of violence," like that supported by the work of Catherine S. Widom (see Widom 1989a, 1989b, 1989c, 1992). Indeed, one of the well-documented risk factors for violence in adulthood is childhood abuse and victimization. In this chapter, we discuss this seemingly straightforward relationship, but we also contextualize the early victimization of the women in our study by using results from the qualitative interviews. Examining context provides a more complicated picture of the childhood lives of these women, and challenges linear or simple interpretations of the nexus of factors that constituted their early lived experiences.

When we compared the reports of childhood happiness with the women's recollection of negative childhood events (e.g., violence), not surprisingly, we found that women who had experienced any of the negative childhood events (ranging from adults' yelling at each other to severe child abuse) were much more likely to report an unhappy or very unhappy childhood.

Shaping Young Lives

In large part due to feminist criminologists (see Arnold 1990; Belknap and Holsinger 1998; Chesney-Lind and Rodriguez 1983; Gilfus 1992), gender has emerged as an important variable when studying the relevance of childhood victimization to violence against or perpetrated by women in adult-hood (Arnold 1990; Brett 1993; Chesney-Lind and Rodriguez 1983; Gilfus 1992; Silbert and Pines 1981). Considering gender problematizes a simple, formulaic relationship between child and adult victimization. Chesney-Lind and Pasko note that "unlike boys, girls' victimization and their response to that victimization is specifically shaped by their status as young women" (2004, 27). Widom, who promotes the "cycle of violence" theory, finds in her more recent work that while "it is clear that childhood victimization has pervasive consequences for criminal behavior and violence . . . patterns of increased risk differed for males and females" (2000, 9). The ways that gender affects victimization, particularly in terms of sexual abuse, were outlined in chapter 1. One salient point was that research that focuses on the gendered nature of victimization finds the rates of sexual abuse experienced by girls to be higher than those of boys. Our examination of childhood experiences begins by considering the different types of negative events experienced by the women in our study.

Our quantitative findings indicate that large proportions of women in our survey experienced negative childhood events, including psychological and physical aggression. About 60 percent said they experienced childhood violence, with about half of all the women classifying violence in their childhoods as severe. It is also apparent that family instability was com-

Table 6.1
Childhood experiences among homeless women (N = 737)

Childhood psychological aggression	66.7%
Minor childhood violence	49.8%
Severe childhood violence	49.8%
Any childhood violence	59.4%
Parents ever married	75.3%
Parents ever divorced, separated, or widowed	64.5%
mean number of times parents divorced (standard deviation)	1.55 (2.05)
Adults yelled at each other	62.2%
Adults hit each other	39.7%
Very unhappy childhood	14.2%
Unhappy childhood	9.9%
So-so childhood	30.7%
Happy childhood	26.4%
Very happy childhood	18.8%

mon, as the majority of women reported changes in parental marital status that included divorce. In addition, approximately two-thirds of the women witnessed their parents yelling at each other, and another 40 percent saw physical violence in the home. In addition to the childhood physical violence, many women were also child victims of sexual violence. Nearly one in three women in our quantitative survey reported vaginal rape victimization before they were eighteen years old. Clearly, violence was relatively common in the lives of these women. Nonetheless, the participants were reluctant to classify their childhoods as unhappy, with the largest percentage of respondents calling their early years "so-so." Victimization, however, did have an impact. Not surprisingly, childhoods filled with violence were not remembered as idyllic. In some instances, women who experienced any one of a series of negative events ranging from witnessing parental violence to experiencing severe violence were more than five times as likely to remember their childhoods as unhappy or very unhappy. For some women, these early experiences marked the beginning of their path to an early adulthood and subsequent homelessness. Our quantitative findings allow us to consider, first, the extent to which the women in our study were victimized both physically and sexually as children and, second, the impact of this childhood victimization on their self-esteem, drug and alcohol use, and adult experiences.

Our qualitative interviews provide a more nuanced understanding of the range of sexual victimizations the women experienced during their childhoods. This range of abuse and exploitation falls along a "continuum of sexualization" (Wesely 2002, 2009). On one end of the continuum are the

Table 6.2

Associations between negative childhood events and childhood unhappiness (percent)

	Unhappy or very unhappy	
	Yes	No
Adults in household yelled at each other	33.9	8.35
Adults in household hit each other	42.7	12.2
Experienced childhood psychological aggression	33.5	24.4
Experienced childhood minor violence	41.1	7.3
Experienced childhood severe violence	40.8	7.9
Experienced any childhood violence (minor or severe)	36.8	5.9

Note: All differences were significant p < .001.

messages that sexualize and objectify girls. These messages can be internalized into identity development, while also being reproduced through daily interactions as girls navigate their worlds. For example, participants in our study recalled hearing from their mothers and fathers that women were only good for one thing, and that one thing did not count for much. Eliza's father told her she should have been a boy, adding: "You're gonna grow up and be a whore and have a belly full of babies. And you're not gonna be any good." Both Ruby and Mo learned that men only wanted women for sex, and that they should use their sexuality for their own advantage. Mo remembers seeing her mother with many different men and reflects on a conversation when her mother told her: "Oh, if you ever want to get a guy's attention, wear this kind of stuff, act this way, do this." Ruby talked about her mother in similar terms:

> She didn't teach me to be—how can I put this—how to grow up. She never taught me how to depend on you and just do for you. She taught me to lay up with the men to get what I want. You know, I thought that's what I was supposed to do. I was supposed to go to bed with all these different men to get what I want. So I just figured that's what [women] were—I didn't know no better. That's what we were supposed to do.

Through these lessons, the women learned that the sexually objectified body was a major part of their value or even their livelihood, but that, paradoxically, this body was the source of their degradation and exploitation. Further, feelings of worth and personal efficacy were chipped away through direct verbal attacks and psychological assaults laced with hate of women.

On the other end of the continuum are physical and sexual abuse. Significantly, sixteen of the twenty women interviewed had endured some sort of physical or sexual abuse as children (at least 12 of the 20 having been sexually abused), with nearly all identifying experiences of emotional abuse or neglect. Many of these instances have already been mentioned or discussed in previous chapters. Rena's story, for instance, was included at length in chapter 2. Her history of violence was extensive, having begun in third grade when she was raped by a school janitor, and continuing with an attempt by her mother to kill her, molestation and attempted rape by her father, and a gang rape when she was fourteen. Similarly horrifying accounts of early sexual abuses and instances of molestation and incest among the participants in our qualitative study were relatively common. For instance, April was first molested by her uncle at the age of two, and by various others until she turned thirteen. Tamara was molested from the ages of seven to nine by "Miss M.," a female family friend; raped by her sister's husband when she was fourteen; and beaten throughout her childhood by her father, usually with an extension cord.

While they were children, these victimizations were frequently denied, even by close family members who should have intervened. Eliza described the beginning of her molestation at age seven or eight by her father:

> And a couple of times my father was drunk and he came in the bathroom while I was getting my bath and he would just look at me. A couple of times, he did reach out and touch me because I was starting to develop. I was a girl. And I didn't like that. I didn't like the way it made me feel and I tried to tell my mother. I went into her room one day and I said, "Ma, I have to tell you something." She said, "What?" I said, "Daddy was touching me." She said, "What are you talking about? He wasn't touching you." I said, "Yes, he was, Ma. He was touching me." And she beat me. She beat me because [in her mind] I lied on my father.

Such a lack of protection was sometimes compounded by blame. Ruby's mother blamed her daughter when Ruby confided her father's molestation: "But she didn't ever believe me. She said I was a whore. She said I deserved it." Ruby's perception developed along these lines: "At the time I just thought that was what I was supposed to let mens [sic] do to me." When she tried to tell her sisters about the sexual abuse, she faced similar reactions:

> *Interviewer:* Let me ask you first: did you tell anyone besides your mom that your dad had molested you?
> *Ruby:* I told my sisters but they were like, I was lying.
> *Interviewer:* Did the police ever get involved, or anything like that?
> *Ruby:* Oh, I wouldn't dare. Oooh, . . . I would have been hurt.
> *Interviewer* [misunderstanding who would hurt her]: Did he threaten you?
> *Ruby* [clarifying]: No, my mom would have beat me. No.

The fact that Ruby would have been hurt by her mother had she reported her father's molestation is revealing. Such reactions also reinforced a victim-blaming mentality that shook these women's already fragile sense of self and agency.

Institutional responses, like that of the criminal justice system, were also rarely reported by the women (this is discussed further in chapter 8). April's abusive uncle got no more than a slap on the wrist from the court system because there was insufficient evidence to sanction him more severely. Dee said she had told her mother about the sexual abuse she experienced at the hands of two teenage male cousins, beginning when she was five or six, and the mother called the police, but that did not end the abuse. "We used to move around a lot," she said, "so that he [one of the cousins] wouldn't know where we were staying. But everywhere we moved, he always knew where we stayed and he always kept his promise" to return and sexually abuse her. In addition to the feelings of vulnerability and fear generated by institutional indifference, the lack of a criminal justice response reinforced the women's distrust in the systems ostensibly designed to protect them.

Beyond their direct victimization, the women were also frequently exposed to violence directed against their mothers or other women in the neighborhood. In addition to the trauma of witnessing and enduring abuse, seeing women mistreated in these ways relayed powerful messages. Tamara states succinctly: "all my life I have seen men beat women." Indeed, the normalization of violence was mapped onto their concept of adult relationships. Ruby comments: "All my relationships I had were very abusive and that's what I thought love was about. I didn't know no better. Any time they would beat me up and—they would beat me up bad and they would tell me later on they loved me. And I'd say, okay. And keep going and going and going that way. And that's like I learned it."

Early Independence

In the qualitative component of this study, the women's average age at leaving home for good was about eighteen; for the women in the quantitative part, it was one year older. This standard transition age belies the amount of shuffling in and out of residences, the early pregnancies and marriages, and the abuse the women experienced while young. Furthermore, the places they lived as children were often not homes in the sense that they provided support or protection. Instead, they were environments characterized by abuse and violence, poverty, loss and dislocation, parental drug and alcohol use and abandonment, and illness. These factors led to transience and displacement beginning at an age much younger than eighteen.

Amelia was shuttled among numerous caretakers for most of her childhood and adolescence. She lived with her father until she was nine, when
he died. She then moved in with her brother for a year and a half; between
the ages of eleven and fifteen, she lived with her grandmother, who then
died. Amelia next moved in with her mother, only to be kicked out at age
eighteen by a new stepfather. It took her less than a year after that to become homeless. Eliza lived with her mother, father, and siblings until she
was seven. Because of drinking and violence between her parents, she then
lived with her uncle for a year. After returning to her parents at age 8, she
was removed by the state and sent to a children's home. After a year or two,
she was sent back home, where she was molested by her father and physically, verbally, and emotionally abused. She was beaten by her mother when
she tried to confide her father's abuse. The parental neglect led her to wan-
der the streets at night, looking for food and care. The first older man she
met at age thirteen or fourteen who fed her when she was hungry became
the father of her first two children. A drug addict, he was abusive:

> He said, "What's your name?" He was real nice; he had a pocket full of money,
> wallet full of money. It was a summer night and I got in his car and I felt safe.
> And we rode over to where we ate. And he actually fed me and I was actually
> full . . . He would feed me. I would be hungry. And I would still go home and
> act like this kid I was. But I'd get hungry. And sometimes there wasn't a pot of
> beans or some bread in the oven and I'd go find it. And he'd say, "You eat?"
> And I'd say, "no." And he'd say, "Let's go get something to eat." He fed me . . .
> But again, it was a nightmare. It was a daydream, waking up from a nightmare,
> because I thought he was just so nice, and then after I gave up my virginity and
> the babies started coming, he wasn't so nice anymore . . . I couldn't go tell my
> mother because I always see her get beat up, her head split open, or her throw-
> ing a frying pan and splitting my father's head, so it was kind of [one] abuse
> upon another.

The childhoods of many of the other women were not dissimilar. The
husband of Junie's mother "hit on her" when she was thirteen, telling her
he was "attracted" to her. When Junie told her mother, she was sent to live
with her grandmother and then her father, who sexually molested her from
the ages of seven to sixteen. After she turned fourteen, the molestation increased, since he had full access to her then. Somewhere along the line, she

was also put in a group home. The effects of sporadic relocation were thus compounded by the absence of healthy adult caregiving, often to the point of violence and abuse. Sara's childhood is illustrative: she left home at fifteen because she was "tired of being a punching bag." While staying at a hotel she had a severe asthma attack, and the Division of Children and Families again became involved, requiring her father to pay for her apartment. She had her first child at fifteen.

One consequence of childhood victimization was that it led some of the women to early independence, or a permanent departure from the childhood home while at a young age. This is consistent with the research, which finds that a substantial proportion of homeless and runaway youth had experienced child abuse (see Janus, Burgess, Hartman, and McCormack 1987; Silbert and Pines 1981; Tyler, Hoyt, and Whitbeck 2000; Whitbeck, Yoder, Cauce, and Paradise 2001). Our quantitative findings reveal that childhood violence was significantly related to the women's experiences of early homelessness: women who experienced minor or severe childhood violence were on average three years younger when they first become homeless, and they were homeless more frequently and for longer periods of time. It is apparent, then, that violence did play some role in the experiences of homelessness for these women, even though most did not identify childhood experiences with violence as one of the reasons they were homeless. This information comes primarily from an open-ended question in the survey instrument asking the women to tell us some of the reasons they left home, the first time they became homeless.

Our qualitative findings reveal that in eight of twenty cases, the women left home in their teens by way of marriage or pregnancy, while six of the women were kicked out or ran away. Diane said:

> It started out at 19 or 18. I mean, I ran away from home, I got out and got married and started having kids just to get away from that. And if I wouldn't have been brought up the way I was brought, maybe things would have been different. Maybe I would have gone to school. Maybe I would have waited to have kids and my life would have been more stable and things wouldn't have happened the way they happened.

Kathleen Ferraro draws on in-depth interviews with forty-five criminally offending women and finds that almost all of them married or became "intimately involved with men as a way out of their parents' homes" (2006, 131). More specifically, she notes that "it was often an experience of sexual abuse or assault, at home or by a stranger, that preceded a young woman's pregnancy and decision to leave home" (132). The women in our study also followed this path away from their childhood homes filled with violence, and headed toward a life filled with more of the same.

Relationship and Family Ideals

The escape from a childhood home via a young marriage or pregnancy is not only motivated by desperation. It also illustrates the pursuit of idealized, romanticized visions of family. For instance, Cammie left home and got married at eighteen, seeing her first marriage as the start of a new family blueprint:

> Because I was very much in love with the guy that I was marrying and I had it in my head that I was going to be able to show my parents that you could have a marriage and make it work and you know, children, and not have alcohol and drugs in the middle of it and do things right. And I mean, I looked at it in a very positive light . . . My thought was, I'm going to show everybody in my family, especially my parents, that you can have a family and you can do it right.

Raphael (2000) addresses the efforts that women who grow up in chaotic environments of extreme poverty or sexual violence make to attain the ideologically normal nuclear family. She references the work of Beth Richie (1996), who found battered African American women trying to make nuclear families work, against all odds. When these relationships became violent, "the physical and emotional abuse so deeply contradicted the women's expectations that they initially deny the seriousness and rationalize the abuse, ultimately finding themselves isolated and in very dangerous situations" (Raphael 2000, 17). Similarly, Cammie (quoted above), endured mental and physical abuse from her husband for years, even as she struggled to realize her dream of having a family and "doing it right."

Eliza recalls: "I only wanted to be a nurse and wife and raise children and live in a normal house, a normal life. And that didn't come." Why was it so hard for hopes to mesh with reality for women like Eliza and Cammie? One theory is that their abusive childhoods replaced words and dialogue with violence: "The ever-present fear of violence prevents children from developing capabilities for hearing and knowing . . . Because of its unpredictable nature, violence interferes with this necessary sense of an ordered world, essential for the development of healthy children" (Raphael 2000, 19). The abusive childhoods experienced by the women in our study were contexts in which the development of the emotional and intellectual skills necessary for successful relationships was absent or disordered. Kathleen Ferraro (2006) notes that sexual abuse, in particular, challenges the healthy development of boundaries and self-protection for girls, and finds Herman's analysis helpful: "The survivor has great difficulty protecting herself in the context of intimate relationships. Her desperate longing for nurturance and care makes it difficult to establish safe and appropriate boundaries with others. Her tendency to denigrate herself and to idealize those to whom she becomes attached further clouds her judgment" (Herman 1997, 111–12).

The feelings and experiences of each individual are located within and intersect with social inequalities and dynamics of power. Kathleen Ferraro pulls together a textured analysis that fleshes out the complexity of these intersections in her introduction to a chapter called "The Social Reproduction of Women's Pain":

> I argue that the emotional and physical pain inflicted by family members on children and adults is deeply embedded in complex structures of feeling that are linked to larger social contexts. Structures of feeling . . . are the subjective feelings that permeate lived experience. This concept mediates between a strictly economic view of subjectivity (i.e., that class position determines personality characteristics), and a psychological or social psychological view that focuses only on individual qualities or interpersonal experiences . . . When daughters feel lonely and unloved and as young women are "swept off their feet" by a violent, abusive man, they align with structures of feeling about romance, masculine power, and overwhelming passion. They are not simply making bad choices or replicating the behavior of their parents . . . People's needs for recognition, meaning and connection to others are channeled and restricted by larger social structures, particularly economic and labor structures. The social control of desire cuts across race, class, and gender boundaries and is also influenced by these axes of domination. (2006, 108–10)

Insights like those of Ferraro (2006) and Raphael (2000) above help situate our quantitative finding that almost as many of the women (86%; $P < .001$) who reported childhood victimization also reported adult victimization. When sexual victimization was included, 92 percent of the women who had experienced childhood violence also had been victimized as adults. In a related vein, we asked the women in our study a series of questions about the controlling, isolating, and abusive behaviors of their current or most recent intimate partners. Women who were childhood victims of violence identified more negative behaviors in their partners. In addition, they also indicated that these negative behaviors occurred more frequently. Although our cross-sectional data do not allow us to presume causality, it is obvious that childhood experiences do influence adult relationships.

Our quantitative analyses found other interesting and significant relationships to childhood victimization. First, childhood victimization was significantly related to other types of adult victimization. For instance, women who had experienced minor or severe abuse as children were more likely to be robbed, pickpocketed, have things stolen from them, and be seriously beaten up, stabbed or cut with a knife, and shot at with a gun. Second, women who experienced childhood violence were also one and a half times more likely to use alcohol, and almost twice as likely to use drugs as adults. Third, women who were victims of childhood abuse were more than twice as likely to feel that the term "depressed" described them very well. Depression was also significantly associated with adult victimization (stalking and sexual or physical assault). It is important to note that the measure of depression in these analyses is a subjective assessment by the women themselves, rather than a clinical diagnosis. Although causal ordering cannot be conclusively established, the association between childhood negative events and the adult experiences cannot be ignored. It is possible, even likely, that the complex nexus of childhood factors we have described plays a role in the level of vulnerability and exposure to risk that facilitates these types of behaviors or victimization.

We discussed the women in this study as perpetrators of crime in chapter 4. It is worth reiterating here that childhood victimization was also related to perpetration. Women who were victimized as children were more than twice as likely to have committed at least one criminal offense. Moreover, women who experienced childhood abuse (minor or severe) committed almost three times as many offenses than women who had not experienced any childhood abuse. Clearly, negative childhood experiences such as abuse have a profound effect on adult behaviors, including both victimization and perpetration.

Table 6.3

Characteristics of adult partners

	No childhood violence	Experienced childhood violence
Would you say your adult partner:		
Has a hard time seeing things from your viewpoint?	2.32	2.63
Is jealous or possessive?	2.16	2.68
Tries to provoke arguments?	1.86	2.29
Tries to limit your contact with family or friends?	1.75	2.00
Insists on knowing who you are with at all times?	2.05	2.54
Calls you names or puts you down in front of others?	1.59	2.01
Makes you feel inadequate?	1.73	2.16
Is frightened of you?	3.69	3.61[a]
Shouts or swears at you?	1.71	2.21
Frightens you?	1.61	2.02
Prevents you from knowing about or having access to money even when you ask?	1.54	1.85
Prevents you from working?	1.30	1.60
Insists on changing where you are living even when you don't need or want to?	1.28	1.73
Threatens you with harming your children?	1.17	1.35
Threatens you with harming your animals?	1.08	1.16
Threatens you with harming your friends?	1.14	1.40
Insists on your having sex without a condom?	1.55	2.07
Prevents you from seeking medical attention?	1.19	1.38
Disappears for a day or days at a time?	1.41	1.71
Leaves you alone without food, money, or supplies?	1.22	1.55
Steals from you?	1.25	1.50

Note: Numbers are mean scores. Responses for all questions ranged from 4 (almost always) to 1 (never). A higher score indicates that the behavior occurred more often.

[a] This figure is an exception and statistically insignificant.

Reflecting on the Cycle

As parents, the women's expectations of themselves and hopes for their children coincided with their impossible ideals of relationships and family. Yet the reality could not have been further from the dream. Of the twenty participants in our qualitative study, fifteen had children, and seven of these fifteen women had had their children removed from their homes. That removal eerily mirrored their own childhood experiences. Some, like Ruby, relinquished guardianship to a relative. Others, like Molly, felt manipulated by family members who agreed to care for the children temporarily, but then kept them from Molly. Children were also removed via more punitive means, sometimes because of the women's abuse or negligence. Five of Sara's seven children are currently in the care of the Division of Children and Families. One of them was removed after Sara threw a plastic bottle at her son, causing an injury to his head that required two staples. Tracy, who worked as a prostitute for twenty-seven years, lost custody of her children to her ex-boyfriend's mother. Examples like these pervade the women's narratives, echoing the instability and dislocation that they experienced as children. Several described their horror and devastation upon learning that their male partners were abusing their children, just as they themselves had been abused. For example, Junie, who had been molested, struggled to talk about the sexual abuse of her daughter by the biological father, Junie's boyfriend of six years. Junie's daughter confided in her mother at the age of eleven, after five years of molestation. Weeping, Junie said: "I went through a lot: being on the street, having kids young, being abused by my mother, my father, and my kids' father. The only thing that kills me the most is what my daughter went through. That's just the hardest thing I ever went through."

Active reactions were typically the technique the women employed to change the situation. Sometimes this meant intervening when the child was receiving a beating, or leaving an abusive partner. Sara's partner tried to hit their children:

> Well, he was my first love. After that first year, he started smoking crack cocaine . . . He started beating on me, sexually abusing me, emotionally abusing me . . . I grew up like that, so sometimes I thought it was normal, that was the way it was supposed to be because that's what happened in our family . . . I dealt with most of it and there have been times when he would abuse the children and I would intervene, instead of him hitting the children, I would take the beating instead. Because I knew how it was being a child growing up abused and it's a scary situation.

Eliza also stepped in and took a beating for her child, and that event led her to leave the relationship:

He pushed me out of the way and he grabbed my baby and . . . he kicked him. And when he kicked him, he landed a kick right in his back and that's when I just snapped. And of course I prepared myself for the worst because I had to throw myself on the chopping block because he was—he kicked my baby and was getting ready to beat him to death. And so I took that licking but after he left, I left.

Eliza identified this as the end of the "cycle" for her:

That's what made me break that cycle. It was something in me that snapped that day. And I pressed charges that day and I wouldn't drop them. And he went to jail. And I never went back again. I never went back to him . . . I was glad I broke that cycle in my life, but still I knew I needed to get some healing from my childhood, because my father used to abuse me verbally very bad as well as hit me. And my mother, too.

It was during these discussions of their children that the women began to invoke the "cycle" concept. The cycle of violence becomes a reasonable explanation for why violence, rage, and despair seemingly cling to victims and perpetrators, their parents, and their children, even when they are motivated to break out of these conditions away. The cycle helped the women in our study understand why, in spite of a sincere desire to protect their children, raise them right, and help guide them into happy adult lives, they failed instead. Mo, whose father beat her regularly, described a time when she was violent to her child: "I've caught myself and there was one instance where I didn't catch myself, and I did lash out at [my son] and I felt really crappy for it afterwards. And right now, I'm going to parenting classes to break the cycle."

For many of us, like Mo, the idea of a cycle of violence is a manageable rationale for the pervasiveness of victimization and abuse, and it includes a solution: i.e., parenting classes. Perhaps more important, the concept brings order, and even closure. Junie says: "I couldn't understand why [my mother] was always hitting me. But then later on, I realized her mother was the same with her." Kathleen Ferraro notes: "There is a commonsensical and scientific basis for the widespread belief that childhood abuse leads to adult problems . . . What is less obvious and more complicated to unravel is how children's experiences in families are linked to broader social dynamics that transcend the intentions and limitations of individual parents" (2006, 108). She adds: "the individualistic focus of the cycle of violence model subordinates political analyses of the family, the society, and the distribution of resources to analyses of pathological behaviors within individual families" (112). By examining context, this chapter has challenged a simple and straightforward understanding of the relationship between a childhood nexus of factors and experiences, and the adult lives of the participants in our study. In doing so, we have provided a more complicated picture of the childhood lives of these women.

Conclusions

A theme in the victimization literature is the relationship between experiences of childhood abuse and adult victimization, perpetration, and other negative outcomes. These relationships exist among the women in our study. Our quantitative findings reveal that women who experienced childhood violence were more likely to report unhappy childhoods. Childhood violence also appears to be related to homelessness, as these women were first homeless at a younger age. Childhood experiences of violence are associated with victimization of various kinds in adulthood: about as many of the women who reported childhood victimization reported adult victimization, too. We also found that women who were childhood victims of violence identified more controlling, isolating, and abusive behaviors in their current intimate partners.

Our qualitative interviews enrich these findings by revealing a nuanced understanding of the range of victimizations that the participants experienced during their childhoods, and the connections among the victimizations and to larger structures of inequality, power, and feeling as the women grew up. It is impossible to unravel completely the interdependent components of the women's childhood experiences and their context. Instead, this chapter has integrated the qualitative findings, to demonstrate how childhood abuses were part of a chaotic upbringing that gave the participants few tools to achieve lasting, healthy relationships and families in adulthood, while also heightening their vulnerability to and risk of a range of victimizations. Though there is a cyclical aspect to the deeply pervasive effects of childhood violence, it is an oversimplification and a mistake to uncritically plug the women's adulthoods into a cycle-of-violence mold. Instead, adult experiences must be seen as part of a larger context that shapes and is shaped by the childhood nexus of factors.

Violence as a Cause of Homelessness among Women

I think the violence and abuse probably led to [the homelessness] because
when I get down in the dumps, I'm always thinking about all that bad stuff.
And then I've been through so much trauma in the last couple of years that
I just felt so beat down and just so lost and I'm asking myself, how did I go
from self-sufficient, taking care of myself, to I was losing everything?
—*Natalie*

The previous chapter illustrated the childhood nexus of conditions for the
women in our study, clearly showing that violence was an enduring part of
their early lives and shaped every subsequent decision and action. Even
with childhoods interrupted with violence and abuse, the women in our
study carried with them idealized notions of what a family and marriage
should look like. Similarly, as noted above, Raphael (2000) found that women
who grow up in conditions of extreme poverty or abuse are incredibly eager
to have a nuclear family, although their early circumstances prevented
them from developing healthy boundaries and skills of self-protection
(Kathleen Ferraro 2006). Childhood experiences of violence, however,
often occur within larger inequalities and contexts of poverty, neglect, loss,
social exclusion and dislocation, substance use, illness, and desperation.
Because of these complex structural, institutional, and interpersonal realities, and despite the women's goals of normal family life in adulthood, they
end up enduring dangerous, violent adult relationships. Indeed, as noted
above, almost the same percentage of women who experienced physical violence as a child experienced physical victimization as an adult. A significant

proportion of women who are homeless may be without housing as a result of these experiences with violence: the quantitative data we collected indicate that one homeless woman in four is homeless at least in part because of violence. Further, some of the women in our study were former shelter residents, who had come straight from the domestic violence shelter to the homeless shelter. Not surprisingly, the relationship between violence and homelessness emerged in one of two areas: child abuse, or violence from an adult intimate partner.

Childhood

In our attempt to understand the paths to homelessness, we asked the women to think back to their childhood memories and tell us if they had ever left their childhood home due to abuse or violence. Almost one in three told us that was part of their personal history. Many of these women grew up in unstable households, where adoptive parents, stepparents, siblings, and friends of the family subjected them to repeated sexual or physical assaults. Childhood memories for many of the women included violence, fear, and betrayal by their own family. For these women, home was not a safe haven where they were protected from the outside world; as a result, they often took the first opportunity they had to leave in search of a better life. This was discussed in the previous chapter, in terms of early independence. As mentioned there, we found that women who experienced minor or severe childhood violence were on average three years younger when they first become homeless, and they had more, and longer, periods of homelessness. Here are two of the responses to the open-ended question in our survey about why women left home and became homeless for the first time:

> At 12 years old I was molested by my best friend's father for about a year, during the time my mother divorced my stepdad and started dating numerous men. In the middle of the night men would come into my room and abuse me. By age 17 years old I was gang raped by 12 boys.

> I felt alone. I got tired of him touching me—then he started giving my little sister money and I knew what was next and I tried to tell her but she said I was lying and to stop and be happy for mama so one night in the middle of the night I left. For good.

For many of these women, sexual victimization experiences frequently occurred while their parents or guardians were preoccupied with drugs and alcohol. One woman recalled her sexual victimization at the hands of her brother. When she told her alcoholic parents, they did not believe her. For others, substance use was central to other family dysfunctions, including violent fights between parents. Another woman responded to the open-ended question this way:

> My father was an alcoholic and used to fight my mother, I used to have to get in the middle of it, and could not handle it. I was 16 years old.

Although sexual abuse comprised much of the childhood violence these women experienced at the hands of family members, a significant number of the women also reported physical violence. One woman recalled that once, when she was pregnant, her father trapped her behind the hot-water heater in their home. Another woman responded:

> There was verbal and physical abuse from both parents. Whenever my mother did things such as being verbally abusive and physically abusive, [it] all came from my father. My father was abusive to my mother and she took it out on us.

Running away from home, even if only temporarily, was a common reaction to the myriad abuses experienced by the women we interviewed. Many of them reported leaving home multiple times to escape abuse from their parents, only to be returned by the police or removed from their home and placed with another relative. Often, the new situation was as bad as, or worse than, their original home. The survey participants talked about experiencing violence so frightening and severe that some left home for a brief period just to find temporary sanctuary:

> Mom would whip me with electric cords. She had abusive relationships and I'd leave so I wouldn't get hurt a lot. Mom was an alcoholic. I'd frequently spend nights with friends so I wouldn't have to deal with it. At 15 she kicked me out.

> I ran away a few times, starting at 14. There was a lot of dysfunction. Domestic violence. Mom alcoholic and abused prescription drugs. Left to be on my own at 17.

I would run away at times. My stepdad was real abusive to my mom (broke her ribs, etc.) and me. He hit me a lot. My mom became an alcoholic. She eventually became abusive to me and my sisters.

Early independence typically exposed the women to even more violence and victimization. Our quantitative data indicated that women who left their childhood home due to violence were 30 percent more likely to experience adult physical violence, and were more likely to experience multiple types of violence, compared to women who remained at home. Survival strategies of prostitution and exotic dancing were also more than twice as likely to occur among women who left a violent childhood environment. This is consistent with the existing literature, which finds large amounts of women in the sex-work industry having experienced child victimization, especially sexual abuse. According to Raphael (2004), in the twenty most recent studies of prostitution, the lowest percent of the women sexually abused as children is a third, with the highest being 84 percent. Within a larger context of gender inequality, limited options for survival on the street target young women for sex work, thus putting girls at even greater risk for harm:

> Survival on the streets of any city is dangerous for a young woman. If she is too young to look for legal work or has too few skills to find work at a living wage, she has few choices other than to find a "hustle" which will generate income for food and a place to sleep. Whether looking for shelter, panhandling, shoplifting, selling drugs or turning tricks, a young woman alone on the streets is often "fair game" for male violence. (Gilfus 2006, 10)

The twenty research studies find an "almost unimaginable level of violence in street prostitution" (Raphael 2004, 100). A study by the Center for Impact Research in Chicago (Raphael and Shapiro, 2001) investigated a sample of 113 women who worked as street prostitutes and found that 20 percent said customers had threatened them with a weapon, 22 percent said they had been forced to have sex, 39 percent reported being slapped, and 33 percent reported being punched. Such high-risk survival options for homeless women are "intricately connected to women's subordinate position in society where victimization by violence [is] coupled with economic marginality" (Gilfus 2006, 13).

Despite these risks, the women in our study typically found leaving an abusive childhood home better than remaining. One woman told us she moved out of her childhood home at fifteen and was legally emancipated.

She was able to get a job and continue school while living with a friend. Other women found different avenues out of their childhood homes. As we noted in the previous chapter, marriage or pregnancy often provided an impetus to escape. One woman said: "My father was very strict. I was terrified of him. I became pregnant and didn't want him to know. I left and moved in with my boyfriend" at about age sixteen.

Such situations contributed to the women's economic instability. Sara, who left home because of severe abuse and had a child at the age of fifteen, said: "but I guess being at the age of fourteen, fifteen years old, you can't fend for yourself, you can't get a job, nothing." The difficulty of supporting themselves at young ages was a major factor in their eventual homelessness, but some still framed this as a choice that was preferable to staying in a violent home. Mo recalled that she became homeless the first time to escape her abusive father:

> I just know I kinda left for a little while and [my father] didn't know where I was for about two or three years. I did that on purpose. I didn't contact no one in my family for a long time . . . In my case, sometimes it was a choice because I didn't want to be found. I didn't want nobody to know me so it was easier to be homeless.

The fact that a young woman like Mo must "choose" between being trapped in a violent home or being homeless raises two questions: What are we offering these adolescent girls? And is choosing between two dangerous and frightening situations ever a real choice? It helps to see these as "structured choices," because "circumstances have limited the agency of these girls at critical turning points in their lives" (Pettiway 1997, xxx). Indeed, within the overlapping and multiple contexts of deprivation, poverty, and social exclusion experienced by these girls in their childhood homes, the move away from violence ought to not be construed as an active move toward homelessness. Instead, it must be seen, quite simply, as survival.

Violence by an Adult Intimate Partner

The early relationships into which some of the women escaped too often yielded more violence. In fact, many of the women we interviewed left their childhood homes as a result of violence, and also became homeless as adults for the same reason—this time primarily because of violent adult relationships. Just over one in five of the women we surveyed were homeless with either their husband or another intimate partner. The women described these companions as drinking heavily, using drugs, and committing violent acts. Approximately one woman in five experienced verbal abuse from her intimate partner, and one in six was physically abused by this person. Eighteen of the twenty women we interviewed had also experienced at least one violent adult relationship.

Intimate partner violence contributed to the women's homelessness through several possible avenues, which frequently overlapped. Some women became homeless with their abuser. Frightened by the man's threats, these women felt trapped with the partner, who tended to be economically unstable. Typically, the partner's financial problems were due to drug or alcohol abuse or unemployment. For instance, Sara says of her ex-boyfriend: "Sometimes he would [help out] but most of the time he wouldn't. Most of his money would go on crack cocaine, and I would have to take care of the bills and the kids and everything." This man was very violent to both Sara and her children. He was arrested numerous times for child abuse and battery against her, but she dropped the charges out of fear. This was not idle fear: he would call Sara from jail to threaten and harass her, and on one occasion he returned home only to beat her, choke her, and hit her son, leaving a bruise on the side of his face. He held Sara and their five children hostage for an entire weekend, at the end of which they finally escaped. Sara was briefly homeless with this man, and he threatened to kill her if she tried to leave him. She says:

> I guess for the longest time, I stayed with him because I wanted my kids to have a family environment. I wanted them to have a mother and a father to grow up with. But he's not really a father for them. And it just got to a point where I was just tired. I was tired of being scared. I was tired of not being allowed to do anything. I was just tired of everything and I had reached my limit with him . . . I couldn't take it no more. And the day after the trial, they TPR'd [Termination of Parental Rights] his rights as well because of his drug problem. And that night he threatened to kill me. He said that he'd already lost his kids, he wasn't about to lose me and so that was just it for me.

This was the turning point for Sara, and she left and went directly to the homeless shelter. Her fear still lingers, however: "When I was with him, I was afraid of when he was gonna beat on us again, and then when I wasn't with him, I was afraid of when he was gonna pop up on me."

While "co-homeless" with their abuser, women described their efforts to keep a job and save a little money. However, the male partner's control of the meager income worked in combination with a passive or purposeful sabotage of the woman's attempts to sustain employment. Cammie's abuser was seen in chapter 5 throwing her across their hotel room after she did not pick up food at Wendy's for him, thereby tearing the rotator cuff in her shoulder. On other occasions, he knocked out her teeth, head-butted her, and broke her nose. She comments: "It was a vicious cycle—it didn't matter how much money I made, I couldn't save the money I made, you know? I was forever giving the money over to him or I was trying to pay the rent."

Roll, Toro, and Ortola's assertion "that domestic violence has a major impact upon women and often results in their becoming homeless, suggesting that many women would rather turn to the streets than face victimization by their partners" (1999, 195) is clearly supported by our study. The few women whose abusive partners had steady, lucrative jobs again faced a "choice" between a violent relationship— which nonetheless provided access to the basic necessities for themselves and their children—or being homeless. Diane, for instance, was severely abused by her husband, which landed her in the hospital several times, generated multiple restraining orders against him, and culminated in his being convicted more than once of domestic violence. Yet his job supported her and their children and, importantly, provided them with health insurance. However, the family's multiple interactions with law enforcement got the attention of social services, and Diane lost custody of her children. Despondent, unsuccessful in her goals to provide and care for her children, and becoming more addicted to drugs, Diane left her abuser and became homeless.

Our quantitative findings and qualitative narratives both show that violence was commonly experienced by women as a precursor to their first homeless episode. Some type of abuse was one of the most common responses to the previously mentioned question about why the women left home the first time they became homeless. Reports of abuse ranged from verbal abuse to severe physical and sexual abuse. Some of the women said:

Abuse. Physical abuse from my children's father. Third-degree burns on my body, kicked down 15 flights of steps which led to hospitalization. A lot of verbal abuse.

I had a man that got out of jail and was jealous and possessive. He tried to burn me up and started the apartment on fire.

I left due to violence, we were arguing for several months leading up to an explosive episode of violence when he was choking me and I decided I needed to leave.

For women who had endured multiple episodes of homelessness, violence appeared to be less central. Later periods of homelessness often included violence; however, equally as often these women talked about economic crises such as losing a job, not being able to afford their rent, and drug and alcohol use by themselves or their partners.

The women themselves pointed out most of the connections between violence and homelessness in their lives. Diane stated: "it's the violence and the drugs and everything that has gotten me to this point of being homeless." Indeed, the effects of violence, both in childhood at the hands of caretakers and in adult relationships with intimate partners, facilitated the women's homelessness in many ways, not the least of which was the erasure of their feelings of value, self-worth, and self-sufficiency (discussed in greater detail in chapter 9). Without these, as Natalie says, "it's hard to get out of the pattern of thinking there's something wrong with you, and then you end up like this and you're like, well, I guess they were right all along. I am worthless, I am useless, I am unlovable." Hayley points out that she resisted homelessness in every way she could, but still ended up there: "Everybody that's in this [homeless] situation, whether or not they want to admit it, has been abused or has abused somebody in their life to get to this point. You didn't get here by your own free will. Somebody dragged you here, kicking and screaming, probably."

Conclusions

The women's accounts of the relationship between violence and homelessness were illuminating but not completely surprising. The hard numbers reveal that women who left their homes due to childhood violence were younger when they first became homeless, were homeless a greater number of times, and were homeless more often in the five years before we spoke with them than women who did not leave home. These facts did not go unnoticed by the women themselves: more than a third of the women believed that their victimization interfered with their ability to get and keep a job, and to find or keep housing. As the majority of women had experienced tumultuous childhoods filled with unspeakable horrors, the decision to leave (or, in many cases, the complete lack of choices) as a result of these experiences followed them right up to the day they touched our lives.

As these women have described, the path to homelessness is fraught with peril and frequently begins early in life. Childhood violence often provides an unstable foundation upon which to build a life and sets the stage for later unhealthy relationships and behaviors. By the time homeless women arrive at a shelter, their cumulative negative experiences have shaped their view of the world, and obtaining a normal life may be beyond their reach. Shelters and shelter workers are prepared to deal with the external issues of being homeless—such as food, clothing, and shelter—but they are likely to be ill prepared for the complex internal issues resulting from years of violence, terror, and betrayal. The barriers to self-sufficiency for these women, who have endured years of psychological, physical, and sexual abuse, are massive and cannot be overcome simply with a place to sleep.

= 8 =

The Criminal Justice Response

> This is what they were saying to me: "In the last 30 days, you've called the police 15 times . . . The next time we come out here, somebody's going to jail, even if it's you." And, I mean, I got kind of mouthy with them. I said, "You're going to take me to jail for what? For calling the law?" You know. —*Cammie*

Among the general population, violence committed by an offender whom the victim knows is reported to law enforcement officials much less frequently than assaults in which the offender is a stranger (Gartner and Macmillan 1995; Maston and Klaus 2005). Barnett, Miller-Perrin, and Perrin note that until the 1970s, police in all fifty states could arrest a domestic violence perpetrator only if they suspected the person had committed a felony or if he or she had committed a misdemeanor in the presence of an officer: "Police responded to intimate partner violence according to policies that protected the privacy rights of families. Police departments traditionally trivialized family violence as non-criminal, noninjurious, inconsequential and primarily verbal 'spats'" (2005, 274). One example of this approach is the 1984 case of *Thurman v. Torrington*, in which Tracy Thurman had her neck broken and was repeatedly stabbed by her husband while a police officer looked on. A review of twenty-five studies (Erez and Belknap 1998) indicates that historically police are less likely to arrest batterers than other violent perpetrators. In fact, Barnett, Miller-Perrin, and Perrin (2005) find that police have often treated domestic violence perpetrators differently than other violent men, failing to arrest some of the most violent, including those who have used guns, knives, or clubs, or who have thrown female partners down flights of stairs (see also Buzawa and Buzawa 2003; Fyfe, Klinger, and Flavin 1997).

Researchers investigating this differential involvement of the criminal justice system have focused on law enforcement response, or lack thereof, and the results have been critical of individual officers as well as of law enforcement in general. Results indicate that police officers were often skeptical of the honesty of victim statements (Buzawa and Austin 1993), and they often held victims responsible for the violence (Davis 1983). Further, arrests were less likely to occur when the offender was an intimate partner (Avakame and Fyfe 2001). Not surprisingly, victims often report dissatisfaction with police response, citing feelings of being blamed, minimizations of the seriousness of the violence, and general police indifference (Stephens and Sinden 2000). Police responses to victims of intimate partner violence mark an important point in the potential pathway to homelessness, as positive responses have been linked to a reduced likelihood of homelessness (Baker, Cook, and Norris 2003).

The research cited above has focused on police-victim interactions among the general population. Little is known, however, about police responses to women who are homeless and victims of violence, particularly of intimate partner violence. Introducing homelessness into the equation of police response also adds the stigma and stereotypes attached to the homeless, and the public's opinions of what services or assistance homeless people deserve. According to Gans (1995), the homeless are feared and often viewed as dangerous because of media images of crimes committed by them (Donley 2008; Snow, Baker, and Anderson 1989). Further, political and media pressure to get homeless individuals out of sight certainly may influence law enforcement perceptions of homeless individuals and responses when they call for assistance. This response is a prime example of how social control agents refer to "social junk" (Spitzer 1975). Recent attempts to criminalize activities most often associated with homelessness, such as sleeping in public places and panhandling, are also indicative of public attitudes toward homeless individuals (National Law Center on Homelessness and Poverty 2009). In addition, many law enforcement officers have extensive experience dealing with homeless people and tend to view them more as perpetrators than as victims. Consequently, the police are often openly hostile to people they perceive as homeless (Wright and Donley 2008). Donley's study of unsheltered homeless people, for example, found that homeless men and women were well aware of law enforcement officers' hostility toward them: "most participants complained of arrests on what they felt were comparatively trivial grounds: 'molesting a dumpster' (dumpster div-ing), 'impeding the flow of foot traffic on a public sidewalk' (sitting on a sidewalk), or 'solicitation of funds without a permit' (panhandling)" (2008, 114). It is not unexpected, therefore, that these attitudes may surface in law enforcement response to the victimization of homeless people.

Most studies of violence against homeless women have discussed the implications of their results for care providers or for the police, but none (as far as we know) has asked samples of victimized homeless women whether their victimizations were reported to the authorities— and if so, with what results. Again, homeless people get less attention as victims of crimes than they do as perpetrators of them, many of which are part of the survival strategies the homeless use to stay alive. An important part of our study, therefore, is an examination of the interaction between victims and the criminal justice system.

Homeless Victims and Reports to Law Enforcement

We begin by looking at the act of reporting victimization to law enforce-ment. As is the case with many sexual assault crimes (Catalano 2004), many of the women (and none of the men) in our study did not report their sexual victimization to the police. The sexual victimization most often re-ported to the police by women was vaginal rape. Though rape was experi-enced at least once by half the sample, only 40 percent of those victims re-ported the crime to the police. Around 30 percent of the female victims reported either oral, anal, or object rapes; fewer reported attempted rapes (22%, 12%, and 15% were victims of oral, anal, and object rape, respectively, and 23% were victims of attempted rape).

We asked the women who said they did not report their rape victimiza-tion(s) to the police to tell us why they had not. Among the many reasons given, the major ones were fear of repercussion from the perpetrator and embarrassment or shame. Some women did not report their victimization to the police because they did not know how to do so. Several such reasons coalesced in the case of Ruby, a participant in our qualitative study, who described being tricked into going into an apartment by a female acquain-tance paid by the assailant. The woman quickly abandoned Ruby in the apartment with the attacker. He threatened Ruby with a knife, sprayed her with Mace until she could not breathe, and forced her to perform oral sex:

Table 8.1

Homeless women's reports of sexual violence to the police

	Vaginal rape	Oral rape	Anal rape	Rape with object	Attempted rape
Experienced forced sex	51 (371)	22 (162)	12 (88)	15 (113)	23 (167)
Among victims, those who reported to police					
Yes	40 (147)	28 (43)	34 (29)	30 (33)	22 (36)
No	60 (224)	72 (112)	66 (57)	71 (79)	78 (128)

Note: Numbers not in parentheses are percents of women; numbers in parentheses are numbers of women (N = 737).

Ruby: He threatened me with the knife. And I was praying the whole time: "Lord, get me home safe. Get me home safe." I got home, I took a bath. I felt so dirty. And I wanted to sleep. My son said, "Mom, what's wrong?" I said, "Oh, nothing wrong, baby. Nothing wrong." I kept it inside for a long time.

Interviewer: Did you tell anyone at the time? Police?

Ruby: No. I was ashamed. It was dumb; it was stupid. Following behind someone else . . . If I go to them they [will] say, "What [were] you doing up there? Why did you go . . . ?" and question me. And I don't have no answer for them. I just followed this girl up there. It was in a rough neighborhood, anyway.

Ruby's response indicates that she felt the police would blame her for going into a stranger's apartment, especially because it was in a "rough neighborhood," which implies she should have known better. This compounded her shame.

Many women reported that they had been using drugs at the time of the victimization or were involved in other offenses; they did not report the rape because they did not think the police would do anything, or because they felt that they would put themselves in legal peril by coming forward. In response to an open-ended question, one woman recalled: "I was using and because I did it [had sex] to get drugs, I did not want to get the police involved." Others indicated that they thought their behavior had played a role in their victimization, and so the crime should not be reported to the police. For instance, one survey participant felt that because she had used drugs with her attacker, she was at fault for the rape and so did not report it to the police. Another woman told us she was too high on crack and was selling her body, so she felt she deserved the sexual assault. One woman did not report her sexual victimization to the police because of previous involvement with them and her subsequent belief that "it wouldn't matter to them" if she was raped. Also highly disturbing is the fact that several women told us that they did not report their victimization to the police because they felt that getting raped was normal. One woman remarked: "It never crossed my mind to call. I didn't see it as violent."

Victims of attempted sexual assault also indicated that because there was no completed act, they did not feel that the police should be contacted. Several women referred to their attempted sexual assault as not serious enough to be reported. One woman said that she did not report her attempted rape because she did not think it would count as rape; since it would be hard to prove an attempted rape, there was no reason to pursue it with the police. Other responses, similar to Ruby's above, included embarrassment that the women had "allowed" something like this to happen to them.

In contrast to sexual victimizations, a greater proportion of both men and women in our sample reported physical assaults to the police. Physical assaults do not carry the same stigma as sexual assaults, and therefore may be more likely to be reported to the police. Among the women in our sample who had been victimized by a physical assault, a small majority (54%) said they had reported the assault to the police; among victimized men, just under a third (32%) reported their assault.

Among the most common reasons women gave for not reporting physical victimization to the police were fear of perpetrator retaliation, dependency on the perpetrator, and not feeling that the incident was serious enough to report. Fear of retaliation is justified, as women who separate from their abusive partners are at an increased risk of further abuse and death (DeKeseredy and Schwartz 2009; Walker, Logan, Jordan, and Campbell 2004). In an open-ended section on our survey, one woman told us she did not report physical assaults by her husband because he threatened to chop her up into little pieces if she told the police. Tracy, on the other hand, blamed herself when her boyfriend put her in the hospital:

> Because I didn't come home when he said and he beat the hell out of me for three and a half hours. He broke my foot, broke three ribs, cracked two, cracked my tailbone, bruised me up so bad, it's unreal. Beat me with a cane, beat me with a broom. And I still went home. Because I know I'm the one that caused it. I knew better, OK? I knew better. That man ain't never put his hands on no woman until he got with me.

Sherie was in an abusive marriage for thirty-seven years. Every single day, her husband committed some form of violence against her. She has had major surgery on her nose, has had doctors put wires in her jaw, and has lost part of her hearing due to the abuse. However, since her abuser's father was the local chief of police, her victimization was ignored, and she remained trapped in the relationship until her husband became interested in another woman (a few years later, she had a stroke and became homeless for the first time at age fifty-nine). Similar attitudes of indifference or even tolerance for such violence were reported by other women. For example, one woman told us that "back in the day," women simply did not report "things like that" to the police. "Women were to be seen and not heard," even when being physically victimized. Other women described learning from previous experience that they did not gain anything by reporting their victimization. One woman told us she did not report an attack "because in the past, the law seemed like it was not on my side . . . Once when I did report it, they treated me so nasty until I left and told them I was better off just being left alone. And now I am all alone because I can't trust no man." Another woman remembered a previous encounter with the police: "They didn't want to do anything when he raped me, so why would they when he hurt me [physically]?"

Indeed, the women in our study often cited prior negative experiences with law enforcement as one of the reasons they did not report their victimizations. Importantly, some also experienced negative reactions from police explicitly because they were homeless. When asked why she did not report her victimization to the police, one woman stated: "Because I was homeless and the police don't care about homeless people. They say it was good that it happened because you living out here like this. That's why I don't trust them."

The narratives of the participants in the qualitative portion of the study reflected that many of their adult attitudes about police were shaped by experiences they had had as children. Diane remembered that neighbors called the police numerous times about her father's violence against her family:

> Everybody in our community knew how he was and so a lot of the people—we didn't have a lot of friends because other parents wouldn't let their kids come to our house. I mean, he terrorized the neighborhood, not just us. The police were called on him several times but he always managed to get himself out of it. Once I remember the police came and he faked a heart attack so instead of going to jail, he went to the hospital. He was very manipulative. He was also very smart . . . So he worked the system rather well.

April was molested by her uncle from age two to age thirteen. The police were called, but as they gathered information, they concluded that there was "insufficient evidence" to pursue the matter. April describes the situation as follows:

I was spending the night with my cousin when I was about 13 and I was mentioning it to her and she made me tell her mom and nothing ever came about it. They called the police, and he got slapped on the wrist by the court system.

In chapter 1, we quoted Eliza, who recalled her childhood neighborhood as one where violence against women was so routine that it was rarely considered severe enough to warrant a call to law enforcement. Eliza saw that when the police were contacted, they seemed to side with the male abusers, who as a result were seldom punished or even reprimanded for their abusive acts. This reinforced the women's feeling that they would never be safe and would never get protection from the police.

Negative interactions such as these are extremely important because they shape the women's future willingness to involve the police in their lives. Among victims of intimate partner violence, satisfaction with police intervention is an important factor in the decision to report subsequent victimizations (A. Smith 2000). Further, positive interactions with police significantly increase the likelihood of reporting violent crimes (Conaway and Lohr 1994). Homeless women are thus in double jeopardy—or worse. Not only are they victims of violence, they are also homeless (and possibly involved with drugs, mentally ill, and nonwhite, as well as almost certainly being poor), and some people believe these facts justify the women's mistreatment.

Our quantitative survey identified some additional factors associated with calling the police. White women were more likely to contact the police when they were victimized; Latina and African American women were less likely to do so. This is consistent with existing research that finds that women of color often face more barriers in reporting intimate partner violence (Potter 2006; Rasche 1988). Women who were separated from their partners were also more likely to call for police assistance when they were victimized than were women living with partners. Homelessness itself also played an important role, with women who had been homeless a greater number of times more likely to call the police.

Women who were sexually victimized by an intimate partner at least once were less likely to report their victimization to the police than were women who were sexually victimized by someone who was not an intimate partner. In contrast, women who were physically assaulted by an intimate partner were more likely to contact the police than women who were physically assaulted by someone other than an intimate partner. What could explain the different patterns? Physical abuse may have resulted in more serious injury and consequent police attention, whereas the stigma of being sexually assaulted by an offender they knew may have prevented women from asking for law enforcement assistance.

Among men, African Americans were more likely to report their victimization to law enforcement than were men from other racial and ethnic groups. In contrast to female victims, the relationship of the perpetrator to the victim did not seem to be as relevant in determining whether or not a male victim would contact the police.

Law Enforcement Response

How did law enforcement respond when women did call for assistance? Historically, police officers have offered little assistance to battered women, in general refusing to arrest men for assaulting their wives, or belittling women seeking police help (Dobash and Dobash 1979; Martin 1976; Schecter 1982). Further, the specific type of response may vary by victim characteristics, with better responses to victims who conform to societal expectations of appropriate victims (Buzawa and Buzawa 2003). Law enforcement responses to calls for assistance from homeless individuals have also been remiss, often tainted by perceptions of homelessness in general and homeless individuals specifically. In one recent study, for example, homeless men reported numerous negative interactions with law enforcement, with at least one officer going so far as to state that his goal was to make the lives of homeless people miserable (Donley 2008). Given this history of law enforcement responses to both battered women and homeless individuals, we might expect that the police would do little in response to a call for assistance by someone who belongs to both groups. However, our study revealed both positive and negative responses by law enforcement to homeless women's victimization.

Given that sexual assault is a highly underreported crime, it is possible that even during interviews and surveys, the women did not reveal the full extent of these experiences in their lives. As reported above, in our study not all victims of sexual assault reported their victimization to the police. The percent of sexual assault victims who did report ranged from a low of 22 percent (in cases of attempted rape) to a high of 40 percent (vaginal

Table 8.2

Police response to homeless women who reported sexual victimization (percent)

	Vaginal rape	Oral rape	Anal rape	Rape with object	Attempted rape
What was the police response?					
See you in person and take a report	71	63	67	68	62
Arrest the attacker or take him into custody	40	34	40	41	35
Refer you to court	30	27	30	32	22
Refer you to social services	49	27	30	29	32
Give you advice on how to protect yourself	22	15	23	15	22
Take you somewhere	31	15	33	24	24
Do nothing	11	29	17	29	22
How satisfied were you with the police response?					
Very satisfied	20	17	33	21	24
Satisfied	31	24	27	24	19
Dissatisfied	19	12	20	12	11
Very dissatisfied	30	46	20	42	46

Note: Questions about police response were asked only of respondents who indicated they had contacted the police about their victimization. Police response options are not mutually exclusive.

rape). When these women did report their victimizations, the police saw them in person and took a report in a majority of the incidents. In other words, the police were doing their job. However, in close to 40 percent of attempted rapes and oral rapes, the police did not even take a report. Arrest of the offender was much less commonly reported by sexual assault victims; further, court or social-service referrals were made in only about 30 percent of the cases. Perhaps more startling is the fact that among women who reported incidents of oral rape and rape with an object, almost a third indicated that the police did nothing.

This variable police response is reflected in victim satisfaction levels. Regardless of type of sexual victimization, a minority of women in our study reported that they were very satisfied with the police response to their calls. This is particularly important for women who are on the verge of homelessness, as a positive police response significantly reduces the likelihood of homelessness (Baker, Cook, and Norris 2003).

Consistent with the quantitative results were the words of the women we interviewed. For instance, Molly, as described in chapter 5, reported being raped anally when two men broke into the hotel room she was staying in while she was asleep. She went to a doctor because of her injuries and did report the attack to the police, but says: "Honey, what could I do except call the police for help? But they never really helped much." As part of being homeless, the women frequently stayed wherever they could to avoid living directly on the streets. As was the case with Ruby's reluctance to report her oral rape in a "rough neighborhood," where the assault occurred was sometimes thought to influence police response. Rena was raped in a crack house:

> I called the cops and the cops didn't do doodley squat . . . you know why they didn't do anything? Because it was a doggone crack house in a crack area. That's why. So they probably say, yeah, she's probably lying. I don't know what that man told them, but when they took the handcuffs off . . . I was too pissed. I say, what the hell good is the police. You know? Really.

Rena's suspicion that the police thought she was lying because her rape happened in a crack house reinforces the idea that, many homeless women, like Rena, do not match the conventions of a feminine, sympathetic female victim (Madriz 1997; Wesely 2009).

Shifting from sexual to physical assaults, we find that about 72 percent

Table 8.3

Police response to those who reported physical victimization (percent)

	Homeless women	Homeless men
What was the police response		
See you in person and take a report	69	90
Arrest the attacker or take him into custody	59	38
Refer you to court	35	17
Refer you to social services	42	17
Give you advice on how to protect yourself	26	24
Take you somewhere	22	3
Do nothing	12	3
How satisfied were you with the police response?		
Very satisfied	32	28
Satisfied	30	38
Dissatisfied	18	17
Very dissatisfied	20	17

Note: Police response options are not mutually exclusive.

of the women and 86 percent of the men in our study reported their physical victimizations to the police. Among those who did make reports, just over two-thirds of the women indicated that the police saw them personally and took a report. By comparison, almost 90 percent of men saw the police in person. It is possible that the greater number of physical assaults by strangers experienced by men accounts for this difference. First, stranger assault (rather assault by an intimate) fits more directly into perceptions of "real" police work and "real" criminals (Barnett, Miller-Perrin, and Perrin 2005). Second, these assaults may be more likely to occur in public places, where police are more likely to be called. Some women, like Cammie (quoted at the beginning of the chapter), experienced punitive reactions from law enforcement when calling the police on an abusive partner:

> The last time I called the police on him just before I left my house, the police officer said, "We checked the record before we came here . . . If we have to come back out here again, somebody is going to jail." Because [my husband] used to—when we'd get to the point where I would call the police, he would take off. So he wouldn't be there for them to lock him up.

Gender differences are also evident when police make arrests. Though the officers suggested to Cammie that she might be arrested instead of her abuser, we found that almost 60 percent of the female victims, compared to almost forty percent of the male victims, reported that when the police came, they took the offender into custody. Court and social-service referrals also happened much more often for women than for men, and women also were more likely than men to be removed from the scene of the crime. However, female victims were four times more likely than male victims to report that the police did nothing when they were called.

When physical victimization was separated from sexual, it became apparent that satisfaction with law enforcement response varied by type of victimization. Women who were sexually victimized were more likely to be satisfied with police response than women who were victims of physical assault.

Some of the women we interviewed interpreted police behavior as directly adversarial or punitive. For example, when Tamara was evicted from her apartment, she felt that people from the sheriff's office arrived without notice or warning to forcibly remove her and her belongings from the residence. In essence, this sent her directly to the streets. While on the streets, Tamara encountered police officers patrolling public spaces like parks to keep the homeless from staying too long:

> But during the day, you don't have nowhere to go. So a lot of people usually hang around shelters because they have little benches out front and you'll go sit on them just to have a place to hang. Most parks—the cops will run you out [of] the parks, you know.

Punitive police reactions made it more likely that women would return to their abusers. Sara had her boyfriend arrested about five times. Even then, he found a way to harass her: "Well, he threatened that if I ever left him he would kill me. When I had him in jail he would call and he would harass me where I was staying at or he would have people come to my house where I was staying at." Because of his threats, Sara was afraid to leave, but several times she was so close to being killed during a beating that she finally did go:

> This will be my fourth time leaving him. The first time I left him, I only had one child by him. I left because he was continuously smoking crack cocaine and he

was beating on me. And moving away from him and in with a friend, but he kept my son and the police wouldn't allow me to take my son, because there's no custody papers. So eventually I went back for the simple fact of my child being there. I left him a second time when I had four children by him. He had threatened to kill me. I tried to take my kids out of the house and he wouldn't let me. I called the cops, told the cops that he was abusive and he had a history of it and I just wanted to go over there and get my stuff and my children and again they told me I couldn't take my kids if he didn't allow it and of course, he didn't . . . so they kind of sided with him. I eventually went back home because I didn't want my kids to go through any more stuff.

The lack of legal protection for Sara led her back into a violent situation, and kept her children there as well. In a better turn of events, the third time Sara left her abuser, the police escorted her out, which enabled her to take the children.

As Sara's circumstances illustrate, the women interviewed in our study had a range of experiences with the police. Any one participant had probably experienced multiple victimization episodes, some of which resulted in a call to the police, and others of which did not; some of these calls may have produced generally positive experiences, while others did not. Cammie described a particularly fortuitous circumstance. A police vehicle had been cruising the area where she was staying in a hotel with her husband, who had kicked her and her belongings out. The first time the police drove past her sitting on the porch at 1:00 a.m., they asked her if she needed help. She responded that she was fine, and that she was just waiting for her partner to pass out so that she could go back into the hotel room and get the rest of her possessions. She told us: "They said, 'Are you sure?' and I said, 'Yeah, yeah, I'm fine. Don't worry about it.' Well, they go ahead and they pull off and the next thing I know he rips the door open and he says, 'Get your ass back in the room.'" After he head-butted her and broke her nose, Cammie ran to call 911 on a pay phone, at which time the cops were circling back:

They pulled up on the back side of the payphone and the police officer took the receiver out of my hand and hung it up. And I mean, [my husband] was coming at me like that, and then he's standing there trying to tell them, "I didn't touch her. I didn't lay a hand on her. I didn't do anything." And the one female cop says, "Is he crazy? Does he not realize we just saw you not 20 minutes ago and you were fine?"

In this case, law enforcement may have saved Cammie's life. In another emergency situation, Sara had just been beaten up by her boyfriend, who this time had dislocated her hip:

> When this particular occasion happened, I had to wait until we got on the city bus, which was very painful, because I couldn't hardly walk. So when we got on the bus, I told [the abuser] that I was gonna ask the bus driver about a connecting bus, but instead I told the bus driver to call the police out. And the police officers intervened on the bus.

The police took Sara to the hospital, and then to the domestic violence shelter.

Categorizing the women's experiences with law enforcement as either good or bad can obscure the ways that some aspects of any one experience were helpful, while others were more harmful. Sometimes the women succeeded in having their attacker arrested, but then dropped the charges. Charges can be dropped for a number of reasons, but most of the women in this study had motivations like those of Sara, who usually dropped the charges because she was afraid of what her boyfriend would do to her after his release from jail. Indeed, even with appropriate police responses to their calls, most of the women we interviewed found legal protections to be ineffectual. Restraining orders, when granted, were often violated. Ruby's ex-husband, for instance, violated three such orders. This did little to reinforce confidence in the criminal justice system.

Considering the variety of experiences with police is especially relevant in the cases of women who had multiple instances of both violent victimization and perpetration in their lives. Recall Rena, whose history of victimization is detailed in chapter 2. She also perpetrated violence and went to jail three times. In one instance, while she and her girlfriend were living in a car, police stopped her for an alleged broken taillight (which she believes was actually fine). Instead, she believes that the police recognized her as someone with a suspended license. At that point, her girlfriend had a crack pipe in her purse, and there was beer in the car. Rena was handcuffed and put into the police vehicle, and she "went into a rage" as she watched the police officer begin to scuffle with her girlfriend:

> I was handcuffed and I kicked out every glass there was out [of] the [police] car. Literally. The car was totaled. He was unable to drive the car and I was almost

out [of] the car with handcuffs. They pepper sprayed me. I have never in my life been pepper sprayed . . . The whole time they sprayed me, I held my breath. When they got done I let go and I went off again. They say, what they hell is wrong with her? They thought I was on acid. I wasn't. I was sick and tired of being sick and tired. I was frustrated. I was depressed. I was—you name it. Stressed and all that just came out . . . I said, "Spray me again, motherfucker. I say spray me again." I mean, I was in a rage. I have never acted like that in my life, so help me God. You know, especially with the cops. Because they could have shot the crap out of me. I mean, I've been in a rage, but with the cops? I had on handcuffs and you know how tight the police car is. I kicked out all the glass. All of it.

Rena was jailed for several months for this episode, and she links her rage to the accumulation of stress, depression, and frustration in her life. When Kathleen Ferraro discusses the lives of the incarcerated women she interviews, she finds in their narratives a clear pattern of criminal justice response:

> These women's stories substantiate the arguments offered by Chesney-Lind, Bortner and Williams, and Gaarder and Belknap, that the criminal justice processing system often fails to protect young women and girls from sexual victimization, but holds them accountable when their own behavior results in harm to others. (2006, 29)

This is aptly illustrated in the case of Rena, who never saw her multiple, brutal sexual victimizations result in any justice. It is only when she became a perpetrator that the criminal justice system paid her due attention. In Hayley's words: "The system isn't working for the people. The system is working for itself." What this suggests is that even when individual police officers or entire departments act in ways that are supportive of homeless women victimized by violence, larger problems in the system fail these women from early on.

Conclusions

Both the homeless and victims of intimate violence are groups that have experienced negative interactions with police, but for different reasons. As a seemingly throwaway population, the homeless are typically noticed only when their presence causes problems, and even then they are seen either as a nuisance or as a population to be feared (Donley 2008). Historically, victims of intimate partner violence and sexual assault have been ignored, or blamed or shamed for their own victimization. The women we spoke with were no different, and for many of them, these experiences occurred before domestic violence—known as the violence that takes place behind closed doors—was recognized as a significant social problem. Their experiences of homelessness and, in some cases, violent victimization led them to believe from an early age that the police looked the other way when there was violence against women in their communities. As they grew up, these attitudes reduced the likelihood that they would report their victimization, and were often reinforced by police responses to them. Consequently, homeless women who live with violence have learned that to survive, they have to rely only on themselves.

Injury, Addiction, and Emotional Problems

I couldn't go [to work] looking like I had just slept on the street. Mentally and physically, I was stressed out. I couldn't sleep fully at night because [I was] scared. So you sleep like with one eye open and one eye closed . . . Every day I was fighting to keep my sanity . . . After dealing with homeless men trying to have sex with me, trying to take my money, talking to homeless women [who are] out of [their] head . . . sleeping in the street hoping that nobody is going to come and kill me . . . [then] to go to work and talk on a normal, average level among my coworkers and my boss—it was stressful.
—*Tamara*

Tamara's story has been woven throughout the narrative of this book. This passage (also quoted in chapter 1) identifies some of the stressors in the lives of homeless women—uncertain arrangements for eating, sleeping, bathing, and the other acts of daily life; the intrinsic hazards of street life; sleep deprivation; crushing poverty; public disdain or even contempt; uncertainty about the future; along with many others—but the ever-present risk, and the frequent reality, of violent victimization is among the most debilitating. Indeed, one of Tamara's everyday worries is how to sleep "in the street hoping that nobody is going to come and kill me."

Maslow's famous "hierarchy of needs" (1943) puts physiological and security needs at the very bottom of the hierarchy, as what he termed primitive or deficiency needs—the need for food, water, excretion, and sleep, along with the need to feel physically safe. Maslow's theory is that if the satisfaction of these lower-order needs is thwarted, higher-order needs for love, belonging, self-esteem, and self-actualization never come into focus. Most people in advanced societies take for granted the satisfaction of their deficiency needs. Not so the poor or the homeless. One need not accept all the details of Maslow's theory to sense the devastating effects that a constant preoccupation with lower-order survival needs might have on a person's self-esteem, general functioning, or overall outlook on life.

Prior chapters have established the frequency, patterns, and severity of violence against the homeless women in our study. Here we explore the consequences of that violence in other life domains. The outcomes explored include the extent and seriousness of injuries resulting from violence; the apparent effects of victimization on alcohol and drug use; the consequences of violence for mental health, emotional well-being, and self-esteem; the effects of violence on women's willingness to accept help or enter treatment programs; and the impacts of violence on lifestyle and survival behavior.

Although violence is a common thread in the life tapestries of homeless women, there is considerable variation in the type, frequency, duration, and severity of the violence they experience. Much previous research has compared victims with nonvictims, but this comparison is obviously crude. A homeless woman who ten years ago was hit by her boyfriend once would qualify as a victim of violence, but her reaction to the victimization must be very different than that of a homeless woman whose partner has beaten her daily for the past 20 years. Some victimization is fairly minor, some is not; some is infrequent, some is a near-daily occurrence; for some women, the experience of violence began last week, while for others it has been an lifelong companion. Before we begin to look at the effects of violence on various aspects of the lives of homeless women, we need to find ways to capture the variability of experience in a parsimonious manner that can be related to outcomes of interest.

Summary Measures of Victimization

Victimization can be of various types. Prior chapters have considered sexual assault, physical abuse, and stalking as the most commonly experienced types of victimization among the women in our study. Obviously, women can be victimized by more than one type, or in more than one way. To capture the variation in the overall pattern of victimization, we created a summary victimization measure (see table 9.1).

To restate yet again one important finding, one in four of the women in our sample report never having been victimized in any way. For the pur-

Table 9.1

Victimization types

	Percent of women	*Number of women*
No victimization	25	177
Sexual victimization only[1]	1	10
Stalking victimization only	1	6
Physical victimization only[2]	27	191
Any two types of victimization	31	226
All three types of victimization	15	111
Totals	100	721

[1]Any form of rape, including vaginal, oral, and anal, as well as attempted rape.
[2]Including only the major violence variables from the Conflict Tactics Scale.

poses of the present chapter, this results in one variable comparing ever-victimized with never-victimized women. As is also obvious, very few women in this sample report a sexual or stalking victimization without also reporting some other kind of victimization. In the vast majority of cases, that "other kind" of victimization was a physical assault. This leads to a second variable, comparing (1) women who were never victimized; (2) women reporting only one type of victimization, almost always physical assault; (3) women reporting two types of victimization, usually physical and sexual victimization; and (4) women reporting all three types of victimization.

In addition to the different types of victimization, other variables that may be related to outcomes include whether the violence was experienced as a child, as an adult, or both; the frequency of victimization (we would expect more frequent victimization to have more serious consequences); the woman's age when first victimized (we assume that a younger onset would be more traumatizing); and the seriousness of the victimization (more serious victimizations are presumably more consequential). These potentially important sources of variation in the experience of violence are discussed below.

FREQUENCY OF SERIOUS PHYSICAL ABUSE AS A CHILD

Many of our questions dealing with childhood experiences involve insulting language, spanking, humiliation by parents, and other relatively minor incidents that occur in the lives of many children. As these are both relatively minor and very widespread, we would not expect them to have much of a lasting impact. To separate these relatively minor incidents from more serious (and probably more consequential) kinds of physical abuse, we focused our analysis on twelve serious indicators of child victimization (e.g., being hit, kicked, burned, cut, or shot at by a parent or sibling; see appendix B for the complete list) and used them to generate a frequency measure.

When respondents answered yes to any of these items, we asked (among other questions), "How often did this happen?" "How often" was recorded on a scale ranging from 1 to 6, where 1 was just once and 6 was "more than twenty times." We recoded the "how often" measure into approximate category midpoints (once = 1; twice = 2; 3–5 times = 4; 6–10 times = 8; 11–20 = 15; more than 20 = 25), then summed across the twelve indicators to generate a measure of the "frequency of serious child physical abuse," a measure that ranges theoretically from 0 (none of the twelve things ever happened to the respondent while she was a child) to 300 (all twelve happened to the respondent, each of them more than twenty times).

Seven respondents received the maximum score of 300 on the resulting scale. Nearly two in five women (39%, or 273 women) reported no serious childhood physical abuse (scoring 0 on the frequency scale). Across the entire sample with nonmissing data on the component variables (N = 708), the mean score was 41.1 (the standard deviation was 63.5), with a median value of 6. Among the 435 women with scale values not equal to 0, the median score was 41. These empirical results suggest two variables that we can use in analyzing the consequences of childhood physical abuse: (1) ever experienced versus never experienced significantly serious childhood physical abuse; and (2) the raw scale scores. To give readers a better feel for this variable, see table 9.2 for the recoded version of the frequency distribution.

Table 9.2

Childhood physical abuse (N = 708)

Frequency of serious physical abuse as a child	Percent of women
No serious abuse	39
1–5 experiences	11
6–20 experiences	8
21–41 experiences	11
42–100 experiences	15
> 100 experiences	16
Total	100

FREQUENCY OF SERIOUS SEXUAL ABUSE

Our questions on sexual abuse (specifically, rape) did not directly differentiate between childhood and adult experiences. Instead, the introduction to the sequence was: "Now I am going to ask you some questions about unwanted sexual experiences you may have had as an adult or as a child. You may feel that some of these questions are disturbing, but I have to ask them this way so that everyone is clear about what we mean." Subsequent questions asked about vaginal rape, oral rape, anal rape, and forced digital manipulation of the vagina or anus. "Yes" answers again generated a long series of follow-up questions, one of which was how many times this experience had happened (another was the age at which it first happened—see below). The summary variable simply adds the number of times each kind of rape was reported, resulting in a variable ranging from 0 (no rape ever—the reported value for 48% of the sample) to 236, the highest observed value. Twenty-two women reported a hundred or more rapes each. Among the women who had been raped (N = 383), the mean number of rapes was 22.7 (the standard deviation was 41.9), and the median value was 4.

As before, we use never-raped versus raped as one variable, and the raw frequency scores as another. The recoding in table 9.3 shows the relative rape frequencies.

AGE AT ONSET OF SEXUAL ABUSE

"Yes" answers to any of the rape questions also generated a follow-up question: "How old were you when this happened (or first happened)?" The

Table 9.3
Women raped in adulthood

Number of experiences	Percent of women in the sample (N = 737)	Percent of women raped (N = 383)
0	48	—
1	11	21
2	8	16
3–5	12	22
6–10	6	11
11–50	7	13
> 50	9	17
Total	101	100

youngest reported age across the four kinds of rape we asked about gives us our measure of the "age at onset of sexual abuse" (age at first rape). As just indicated, 48 percent of our respondents have never been raped, and a 20 percent of the women who had been raped declined to reveal the age at which this first happened, so we have age-at-first-rape data for 305 women (80% of those who had ever been raped). The youngest reported age at first rape was one year; forty-four women reported having first been raped when they were five or younger. The mean age was fifteen years (the standard deviation was 10.1 years); the median was thirteen. The latest first rape occurred at age sixty-two. We use the raw "age at first rape" in subsequent analyses, but readers can get a good feel for the relative frequencies from table 9.4.

FREQUENCY OF ADULT PHYSICAL ABUSE

Using basically the same indicators and procedures described above for serious physical abuse as a child, we created an index of the frequency of serious physical abuse as an adult, using the nine "major violence" items from the Conflict Tactics Scale (see appendix B). The frequency of each type of violence was recorded on a scale of 0 to 6; scale values were recorded to approximate interval midpoints (see note 3 above), then summed across the nine items. The result is a scale that varies empirically from 0 (no serious physical abuse as an adult, the value for 34% of the sample) to a maximum of 225 (the median score was 4; median for scores other than 0 was 19; mean score 26; standard deviation 44.2). As before, this generates two variables for the analysis of consequences: never- versus ever-experienced adult physical abuse, and the raw scale scores. The recoded frequency distribution in table 9.5 indicates comparative frequencies.

Table 9.4
Age at first rape (N = 305 raped women)

	Percent of women
Age 5 or younger	14
Age 6–10	23
Age 11–15	25
Age 16–21	18
Ages 22–29	11
Age 30 and older	9

Table 9.5

Adult physical abuse

Frequency of serious physical abuse as an adult	Percent of sample (N = 707)	Percent of abused women (N = 464)
0 occurrences	34	—
1–5 occurrences	18	28
6–20 occurrences	16	24
20–50 occurrences	13	20
51–100 occurrences	11	16
> 100 occurrences	8	12

SERIOUSNESS OF ADULT PHYSICAL ABUSE

Finally, women who reported any instance of serious adult physical victimization were asked how many of these victimizations caused injury, and how serious the injury was. We multiplied "how many" by "how serious" to create a scale from 0 to 9. Women who were never victimized or who had missing data on the component injury indicators were excluded (N = 229, or 31% of the total sample). Among the remaining women (N = 508), a score of 0 on this measure means that they were either victimized but never injured, or injured but with all injuries reported as "not serious at all." At the other extreme, a score of 9 means that the woman was injured "many times" as a result of her physical victimizations, and that those injuries were all reported to be "very serious." Numbers between 0 and 9 thus capture variability in the frequency and severity of injuries experienced as a result of physical victimizations, which we treat here as a measure of the aggregate seriousness of the physical abuse suffered by these women.

Among the 508 women who had been physically victimized and who reported their injuries, 39 percent reported no injuries or no serious injuries, and 12 percent reported many injuries, all of them very serious. The mean score on the scale was 2.9; the standard deviation was 3.1; and the median score was 2. Table 9.6 gives the full distribution as recoded for analysis purposes.

The bimodal nature of the distribution is worth noting. Abused homeless women tend to be either not injured at all (or not seriously injured), or to be repeatedly and seriously injured. The moderate scale values are relatively empty compared to the two extremes.

Table 9.6
Seriousness of abuse scale (N = 508)

Scale value	Percent of women
0	39
1–2	16
3–4	17
5–9	28

Injuries Suffered in Violent Victimizations

Obviously, the most direct consequence of violence is that just discussed—namely, injury to the self (or, in the extreme case, death—which of course is not captured in our data). Of the homeless women in our study, 25 percent said they had never been physically victimized; 26 percent had been victimized but not injured; 12 percent had been victimized and injured, but not seriously; and 37 percent had been victimized and seriously injured. Thus the most common experience was to have been seriously injured in at least one physical assault.

Of the women who had been victimized (and who answered the questions about injury), 65 percent said they had been injured at least once in those victimizations (20% just once, 26% "a few times," and 19% "many times"), and of those who had been injured (N = 355), 44 percent described their injuries as very serious, 31 percent as somewhat serious, and the remaining 25 percent as not too serious or not serious at all. More than half (56%) of the reported injuries were said to have required medical attention, with the percentage requiring medical attention increasing sharply with the seriousness of the injury: 87 percent of the injuries described as very serious required attention, mostly in the emergency room; only 12 percent of the injuries described as not serious at all required attention.

What victimization experiences predict whether the victim is injured, and the seriousness of the injury or injuries? Pretty much all of them do. When we correlated the summary victimization measures (ever versus never a victim; number of types of adult victimization; seriousness of childhood physical abuse; rape histories; age at first rape; and frequency of adult physical abuse) with the recoded "seriousness of injury" scale, we observed statistically significant correlations in five of six cases, with the magnitudes of the significant correlations ranging from .25 to .88. Age at first rape was not significantly related to the summary seriousness measure, but everything else was—with particularly significant correlations with ever having been a victim and the frequency of adult physical abuse. The general finding, then, is hardly surprising: that any increase in the frequency or seriousness of victimization, whether as an adult or as a child, increases the likelihood of serious injury resulting from the victimization.

It is also of some significance that several of the summary victimization measures are also significantly associated with self-reported physical health. In particular, having been victimized, the frequency of adult victimization, the number of types of victimization, and the severity of abuse were all associated with worse physical health.

Alcohol and Drug Use

As discussed previously, our measures of alcohol and drug use and abuse are not ideal. Respondents who had not had a drink in the previous year were not asked most of the alcohol questions; the drug questions were likewise skipped for those who had not used illegal drugs in the previous year.

The one alcohol question posed to all respondents asked whether it was very, somewhat, or not true that "I drink too much." Only 12 percent said that the statement was very or somewhat true of them. Responses to this question, however, were significantly correlated with number of types of adult victimization, all versions of serious childhood physical abuse, frequency of sexual victimization, and frequency and seriousness of adult physical abuse. None of these correlations was strong. In contrast, whether respondents reported having had any drink of alcohol in the previous year was fairly strongly and significantly correlated with every summary measure of victimization except age at first rape. These correlations ranged from weak to fairly robust.

Finally, among those who had used alcohol in the previous year, most measures of the seriousness of their alcohol abuse were significantly correlated with most (although not all) measures of the seriousness of their victimization. Women with more serious and more frequent histories of physical and sexual abuse were also more likely to say that:

- Drinking has created problems between them and their partners.
- They had gotten into trouble at work because of their drinking.

- They had lost a job at some point because of their drinking.
- They had neglected their family obligations for two or more days because of drinking.
- They had tried to cut down on their drinking but had failed.
- They thought of themselves as someone who had a drinking problem.
- They had been in treatment one or more times for their drinking problem.

In general, our measures of childhood physical abuse and age at first rape were less likely to be correlated with these alcohol outcomes than the other summary measures were. And while most of the significant correlations were of modest magnitude ($r \sim .10$), many were substantial. The strongest and most consistent predictor was ever having been victimized as an adult, which was significantly correlated with every alcohol outcome we examined.

Much the same is true of drug abuse. Twenty-eight percent of the respondents admitted to illegal drug use sometime in the year before their interview. Use in the past year was significantly and positively correlated with all summary measures of victimization experience except frequency of sexual abuse and the seriousness of adult physical abuse.

Among the women who had used drugs in the previous year, most measures of the seriousness of drug abuse were correlated with most summary victimization measures: frequency of use, how often the respondent was high on drugs when out in public, unsuccessful attempts to cease use, thinking of oneself as a person with a serious drug issue, and having been treated for drug abuse. Frequency of sexual abuse was not related to any of these indicators; age at first rape was significantly related to only one; and, interestingly, no victimization indicator was significantly related to drug overdoses. But as with alcohol abuse, for the most part there was a clear tendency for drug problems (however measured) to increase with the frequency and seriousness of victimization.

Causal inferences from cross-sectional data are admittedly hazardous, but it is hard to avoid the conclusion that a great deal of the alcohol and drug abuse observed among these women is a direct consequence of the victimization they have suffered. Marion said: "I was always sad and I started drinking." Rena, whose story was related in chapter 2, is unambiguous about the matter. Recall her words:

When I got raped, I felt like shit. I felt like shit and I felt like, "Why me?" I was mad with the Lord. I would say, "Why me, why me, why me?" With all these women running around giving it away free, why me? So that's when [I started], you know, the drugs, the alcohol.

The rape Rena is describing happened when she was nine or ten, in the third grade A little later, she admits: "That's why I drug and drink—from being depressed." In addition to her lifelong history of physical and sexual abuse and her persistent alcohol and drug problems (she has been in and out of rehab more times than she can remember), Rena has perpetrated violence and made multiple suicide attempts.

Mental Health, Emotional Well-Being, and Self-Esteem

Various combinations of victimization, homelessness, and other traumatic life events led the women we interviewed to feel inconsequential, worthless, and alone. These feelings were not only reinforced on a daily basis as the women tried and failed to get support and attention, but fed upon themselves, leading the women to be increasingly emotionally disconnected, depressed, and ultimately apathetic about their circumstances. This apathy often precipitated or perpetuated their homelessness.

Feelings of isolation sometimes came on the heels of a major life crisis. It was not unusual for there to be at least one family member who helped or cared for the woman, and the loss of that person and the resulting grief often started her down a spiral of despair and confusion. Major losses also often worsened situations that the women were experiencing, like violent victimization. Rena was abused by every family member except her grandparents, who raised her for a time. When they died when she was sixteen, she says: "it's like I died." Now in the homeless shelter, she says: "sometimes I feel like I'm alone, and that kind of just put me down." Natalie moved to the city where her sister lived to care for her when she got cancer. After the sister died, Natalie was unsure how to continue with life: "And, I don't know, something just happened to me. I just got so lost, so long, that I didn't feel like I belonged nowhere, didn't have nobody, didn't know what to do." Such losses made the women more vulnerable to predatory outsiders, which facilitated their homelessness. Cammie's life events illustrate this:

In a four-year period of time, my youngest son got killed, my husband got killed, my mother died, my oldest half-sister died, and my baby sister died. And I kind of lost my bearings. In all honesty, I think I had a nervous breakdown and every time I thought I was trying to—every time I was strong enough to get back on my feet and deal with life again, somebody else would die and it just kinda, you know, it kinda destroyed me . . . Well, then I met this guy and he got into my life and he basically drained me dry. And then I couldn't afford my house payments.

Marion, who was frequently beaten up by her partner, says: "you get to feeling like nobody wants you." This feeling was exacerbated when her parents and brother died: "So after that, seems like after my parents died— both my parents died and my brother died, I just felt lost and that's when I started having anxiety attacks . . . I started missing a lot of work. So I quit and I [with]drew the money I had, and I went to the mental hospital for the first time then."

Feelings of being uncared for and alone were extremely common as the women struggled with conditions like those described above. Of course, homelessness only increased such negative feelings. Tracy, who worked as a prostitute for twenty-seven years and has been repeatedly beaten and raped, says: "I don't have nobody. I'm a loner . . . Basically, I've lost everything I've ever had because of stupid shit." Rena says: "I feel like nobody cares." During a discussion about homelessness and abuse, Tamara commented:

Being homeless is abusive [in] that people look down on you. They look at you as dirty or someone bad. They don't look at you and say, well, maybe they had a problem, maybe they house burnt down, maybe they had too much pride to live with they family, maybe they trying to do it on they own. They don't look at that. They look and say, wow, look at this. This person don't want to work. This person is lazy. This person just want to be a menace to society.

Tamara pointed out that even workers in some shelters have these attitudes: "When you go into most shelters, the women that work there look at you the same way the ones on the street look at you . . . They talk down to you. They talk to you like you a dog. They treat you like a dog."

Such feelings intensify a sense of worthlessness that often translates into unhealthy choices or indifference to self-preservation. Marion became a drifter on the streets with a general emotional disconnect and inertia:

I was scared that I—this was the way I was going to live for the rest of my life. That this was it, you know, and I didn't know how to survive. I was lost. I didn't know where I was. I had mental issues, you know? Like I couldn't think clearly. I was getting forgetful and I was tired. I would go and sit in parks, sit on the grass all day.

The miasma of oppressive factors, then—including loss, grief, violence, and especially homelessness—leads to continued feelings of worthlessness and even apathy about well-being. It seems difficult for the women to care about themselves when those who purport to love them abuse them, and society views them as throwaways.

Elevated levels of mental illness of all sorts and degrees of seriousness are commonly reported among samples of the homeless, especially samples of homeless women. After she was molested repeatedly during childhood, Tamara created her own make-believe world in order to cope. She continued to withdraw into this world well into her teens. At a young age, following the molestation, she began seeing a psychiatrist and was misdiagnosed as mentally retarded and schizophrenic. Only later did it emerge that she was actually suffering from post-traumatic stress disorder and depression due to the sexual abuse she had endured. It is surely a plausible hypothesis that one source of the elevated psychiatric disease observed among homeless women is a lifetime of physical and sexual abuse. This hypothesis receives strong support in our data, as the major measures of psychological functioning and mental illness are correlated with virtually all the summary victimization measures, usually at levels well beyond those observed for alcohol and drug abuse.

To give readers a better sense of what these patterns of correlation mean, let us first consider one of the strongest correlations uncovered in this analysis, the correlation between rape experiences and answers to the question, "Has any health professional, counselor, social worker, or other clinician told you that you have a psychological or emotional problem, or that you are mentally ill?" A positive answer to this question, in conjunction with actual treatment histories, is sometimes taken to be the single best indicator of mental illness, and in our data, it is correlated with lifetime rape experiences at $r = .346$, a very strong relationship in data of this sort. Table 9.7 shows the cross-tabulation of the two variables.

Note first that in the total sample, 36 percent have been diagnosed as

Table 9.7
Relationship of mental illness and rape (percent of women in the sample)

| | \multicolumn{7}{c}{*Number of times raped*} | |
	0	1	2	3–5	6–10	11–50	>50	Total
Ever been told you are mentally ill?								
No	81	61	58	54	50	33	35	64
Yes	19	39	42	46	50	67	65	36

mentally ill, a figure highly consistent with other studies of homeless women. Among women who have never been raped, only 19 percent have been diagnosed as mentally ill; among those raped only once, the number jumps to 39 percent. (For those raped more than once, the figure is 49%.) Additional rapes are linearly associated with increases in the percentage diagnosed as mentally ill, but the two big jumps in mental illness are in the transition from none to one rape (a 20-point increase in mental illness diagnoses) and in the transition from between six and ten to more than ten (a 17-point increase). This is compelling evidence that being raped is profoundly deleterious to mental well-being, and being raped repeatedly (ten or more times) is even more so.

The correlation between the two variables in table 9.7 was the strongest uncovered in our analysis of the homeless women's mental health. But several additional correlations were substantial. First, having been told that one was mentally ill was significantly correlated with every summary measure of victimization frequency and seriousness, except age at first rape, with correlations ranging from .16 to .35. And second, outpatient treatment episodes for mental illness were also significantly correlated with every summary measure of victimization except frequency of sexual abuse and age at first rape, although these correlations were not as strong. Interestingly, psychiatric hospitalizations were not correlated with any of the victimization measures except number of victimization types, and then only weakly—a clear exception to the strong patterns shown on other mental health indicators. Thus, mental health diagnoses and outpatient treatment episodes are clearly more common among the physically and sexually abused than others; psychiatric hospitalization is not.

There are also fairly strong relationships between most of the summary victimization measures and the answers to a series of questions about psychiatric symptoms. The introduction to the questions was: "now I am going to read you a list of terms, and for each one I mention, I want you to tell me if that term describes you very well, somewhat, or not at all." The terms were depressed, anxious, tense or uptight, out of control, suicidal, or confused. Table 9.8 shows the correlations between these symptom measures and a selection of our victimization indicators.

Several important points are clear from this table. First, virtually all of these correlations are statistically significant (the .04 correlation between abuse severity and feeling suicidal is not; the .08 correlation between childhood abuse and feeling suicidal is borderline), but some are clearly larger and more important than others. Second, as in most previous analyses, our measure of abuse severity (essentially, the degree of injury sustained as a result of victimizations) is only weakly correlated with symptoms. It is apparently the fact and frequency of victimization, more than the degree of injury sustained, that leads to adverse psychiatric outcomes. Third, the sense of being out of control is only weakly correlated with the victimization measures. This implies that all homeless women are more or less equally likely to feel that their lives are out of control, regardless of whether they have been abused and victimized. The same is true of feeling suicidal, with the important exception that women who have been raped are substantially more likely to think about killing themselves than are women with no history of rape. Finally, with the exceptions noted, all measures of victimization experience are fairly strongly correlated with feelings of depression, anxiety, tension, and confusion.

Table 9.8
Correlations between psychiatric symptoms and victimization measures

Victimization measure	Depressed	Anxious	Tense	Out of control	Suicidal	Confused
Ever victimized	.25	.22	.25	.07	.07	.19
Number of types of abuse	.27	.26	.28	.11	.12	.21
Ever abused as a child	.29	.26	.27	.11	.08	.24
Ever sexually abused	.26	.20	.26	.14	.16	.25
Ever been raped	.26	.22	.25	.14	.20	.24
Ever abused as an adult	.24	.24	.23	.10	.13	.20
Abuse severity	.17	.16	.16	.10	.04	.16

Given the associations with mental illness symptoms and diagnoses, it would be remarkable if the self-esteem of these women were not also affected by their abuse histories, and the quantitative data bear this out. Our questionnaire contained the ten-item Rosenberg self-esteem index, a scale that ranges in our data from 12 to 40, with a mean of 29 (and a standard deviation of 5.4). Correlational analysis confirmed that all the summary victimization measures were related (fairly strongly) to self-esteem, and in the expected direction (the greater the woman's victimization, the lower her self-esteem)—with age at first rape again the exception. For the women we interviewed, childhood and adulthood experiences of violence and abuse also played a major role in their development of low self-esteem; many actually used the phrase "low self-esteem." Dee was first raped at age five or six by her two teenage male cousins:

> *Dee:* He [one of the cousins] was baby-sitting us while my mother was at work. I guess she trusted him with us and I remember my brother was young, he was like a baby. But he would usually have us make a tent and he would play like he was daddy or something. And he would sit up there and have sex with us while my brother would watch. He would have my brother watch it.
> *Interviewer:* And he would actually try to have intercourse with you?
> *Dee:* He did . . . I used to try to talk to [my brothers] about what happened and my oldest brother, he laughed at me and told me that I lied . . . [My cousin] always used to hold me by one leg over the banister, and I remember seeing a glass table and he would tell me that if I was to ever tell what happened that he would drop me and I would die.
> *Interviewer:* On the glass table? That probably scared you a lot. That was when you were pretty young . . . How did you deal with that as you got older? I mean, how did it make you feel about yourself?
> *Dee:* Low self-esteem. It took me a while to let my husband touch me.

Diane, who was called "worthless and no good" and told she would "never amount to anything" by her father, say: "it's taken me like that last few years to get my self-esteem back." Mo recalls: "I absolutely hated myself." She felt her mother did not want her, and her father continually "threw that up in my face." From childhood, Natalie felt she was "ugly and unloved." Marion says she had "no self-value." Sara explains her first relationships with men: "I guess I have a real low self-esteem, so I guess I was just trying to get affection from anywhere I could, because I wasn't getting it from my father or my parents. So I guess when the other two guys showed me affection, I just kinda clinged to it." In adulthood, abusive partners echoed the same messages these women had gotten in childhood. Cammie's husband, for instance, told her she would never be good enough. April, who was raped by her uncle, "figured no one would want me then." These sentiments of worthlessness pervade the women's narratives. Their self-esteem was chipped away at by their childhood experiences, and the adult circumstances they endured only continued the process.

The continuing effects of low self-esteem in the women's adult lives include a lack of interest in life, sometimes to the level of thinking about or trying to commit suicide. Eliza states: "I said, 'Lord, if you can hear me, change me. Bring something into my life or just take me because I'm tired.' I was just tired. I was tired of paying my rent and men coming in, just taking my body . . . and just kind of devaluing me." Hayley is unsure of who she is and claims to have multiple personalities. She expresses numbness and lack of hope about her future, and she has threatened to kill herself and her children so that they no longer have to deal with abuse and pain. When asked if she ever felt afraid on the streets, she laughed and said: "What are they gonna do, kill me? I'm already dead. You know what I'm saying. I mean, how much further low can you get? How much further down can you go? There is no other place to go when you're there."

Whether the women in our study ever tried to kill themselves is certainly an unambiguous indicator of emotional instability (a stricter criterion than having thoughts about such things or "feeling suicidal"). As we have mentioned, Rena attempted suicide several times. Tracy also tried to kill herself by swallowing thirty Tylenols while she was already in the hospital. Remarkably, of those in the quantitative portion of our study who answered the question about ever trying to commit suicide (N = 686), 29 percent reported at least one suicide attempt, and 14 percent reported more than one. Those figures speak volumes about the desperate circumstances in which homeless women regularly find themselves. Suicidal behavior was significantly and pretty strongly correlated with virtually all of our summary victimization measures, even age at first rape. Several of these correlations exceeded .3, and the correlation with rape experiences exceeded .4.

Help-Seeking Behavior

Are battered, abused, and victimized homeless women able to seek professional help in coping with their victimization? At the end of the sequence of questions about adult physical victimizations, we asked, "Did you ever talk to a psychologist, counselor, social worker, or any other type of mental health professional about this incident [these incidents]?" We asked this question only of those reporting at least one adult physical victimization, but the percent who said they had talked to a professional about their victimization increased with the frequency of adult abuse, the number of types of adult victimization, all measures of childhood physical abuse, sexual victimization as a child or an adult, and the number of rape experiences. Many of these correlations were strong. Thus, of the summary victimization measures, the only ones not related to this form of help-seeking behavior are age at first rape and severity of abuse. Victimized homeless women do reach out for professional assistance in coping with their abuse; the more they have been victimized, the more this is true.

Generally speaking, however, they do not reach out to the police, at least not in response to sexual victimization. Each of the five questions about rape and attempted rape was followed by the question, "Did you report this experience [any of these experiences] to the police or other legal authorities?" Majorities ranging from 60 percent to 78 percent said no, and with only a few exceptions, none of these five questions showed much of a relationship to any of the summary victimization measures.[1]

One criticism leveled against the health care system by advocates for the victims of domestic violence is that medical personnel sometimes treat women's traumatic injuries but do not ask about the source of those injuries. Homeless women in our study who said that they had been injured at least once in an adult physical victimization and had sought medical assistance for the injury (N = 267) were asked, "Was there any discussion about the source of your injuries with any of the medical personnel who treated you?" Two-thirds of the women said yes, and the tendency to say yes increased significantly with most of the summary victimization measures.

1. With five "did you report" questions and eleven raw and recoded summary victimization measures, we examined fifty-five correlations in this analysis, of which only six reached the threshold of statistical significance. Moreover, the six significant correlations showed no interpretable pattern—that is, they were not all found for one type of rape, or for one or a few of the summary measures.

A final relevant question sequence for this discussion began by asking respondents, "Which of the following people, if any, have you ever talked to about your experiences with violence?" The number of people mentioned was correlated pretty strongly with all the summary victimization measures (age at first rape was the exception once again).

Krishnan, Hilbert, and Van Leeuwen have pointed out that research on help-seeking behaviors of abused women is limited. While their study was based on women in a domestic violence shelter in a predominantly rural community, the point generalizes to help-seeking behaviors of homeless women in predominantly urban settings as well:

> The decision whether and from whom to seek help is often a complex one for women in abusive relationships. Isolation from family and friends, fear of retaliation from and escalation of abuse by intimate partners, and economic considerations often dictate and compound this decision . . . Extreme physical isolation, limited availability and access to appropriate social and health services, patriarchal family structures and views, and strongly held religious beliefs often complicate help-seeking . . . In addition . . . lack of knowledge and information about available services and familial and cultural barriers often discourage appropriate help-seeking. (2001, 28)

Considering the fear, isolation, extreme poverty, and probable lack of knowledge about available services characteristic of abused homeless women like the ones in our study, one might expect their help-seeking behavior to be especially limited. Yet except for reporting victimizations to the police, this does not appear to be the case. Although the majority of victims who answered the question about discussing victimization with a psychologist, counselor, or other mental health professional (N = 509) said they had not done so, the tendency to discuss victimization increased with its frequency and seriousness. Most of the women injured in victimizations talked to medical personnel about the source of the injury, and this tendency too increased with all the summary victimization measures. And a large majority of victims (71%) found at least someone to talk to about their experiences with violence (including family and friends, 59%; law enforcement, 46%; medical or mental health professionals, 42%; shelter staff, 38%; and minister, priest, or other clergy, 25%), with the tendency to have done so also increasing with most summary victimization measures. The hypothesis that help-seeking might be difficult for the victimized homeless women in our study is not supported.

Consequences for Lifestyles

Our final set of questions relevant to this chapter is how victimization affects lifestyles. Are victimized women more concerned about their personal safety? More likely to carry a weapon for self-defense? Do they spend more time hanging out with people who are drinking or using illegal drugs? Are they more likely to panhandle, derive income from illegal sources, or work as a prostitute or stripper? Do they have more or fewer friends? Are victims of sexual and physical assault also more likely to be victims of robbery and other crimes against property and person? Are they more likely to commit crimes themselves? More likely to have served time in prison or jail? How, in short, do the frequency and severity of a woman's victimizations effect other aspects of her daily life? Interestingly, the answer proves to be: in just about every possible way.

Most homeless women in our study (55%) say they are "very concerned" about their physical safety, and 21 percent say they carry something with them "to defend yourself or to alert other people" at least from time to time. Concern with personal safety is positively and significantly related to five of the six summary victimization indicators; carrying something for self-defense is positively and significantly related to ten. The more frequently and severely a woman is victimized, the more wary and self-defensive she becomes.

Alas, victimization experience also seems to stimulate risky behavior. We asked these women how often they spend time with people who are using drugs. Nearly one in four does this frequently or occasionally; and the tendency to do so increases significantly with nine of the eleven summary indicators. About 5 percent of our respondents report income from illegal sources (mostly drug deals); 7 percent report panhandling income; 11 percent say they have worked as a stripper or exotic dancer; and 13 percent report having worked as a prostitute. Sex work of all sorts, panhandling, and hanging out with people doing drugs are all high-risk behaviors. These four behaviors times six summary indicators produce twenty-four correlation coefficients. Setting aside age at first rape, which is not correlated with anything, the majority of these correlations are significant. Thus, women with the most extensive victimization histories also engage in behavioral patterns that are likely to result in their being victimized again.

We also asked the women in our study how many close friends they have. More than a third have none, and another fifth have "just one," so no friends or only one friend is the majority experience. Many women (40%) have "a few" friends. Hardly anyone (5%) has many. We hypothesized that a lifetime of abuse and victimization, coupled with the consequent effects on mental health and self-esteem, might reduce a woman's ability to make and sustain close friendships, but this does not appear to be the case. The number of friends was only significantly correlated with one of the six indicators, and only weakly at that.

Almost half (45%) of the women in our sample have spent time in prison or jail; slightly more than half (51%) have committed crimes; and the large majority (72%) have been victimized by crimes other than physical and sexual assault (being robbed, having their pockets picked, being stabbed or shot at, etc.) That victimization is very strongly correlated with all our summary indicators except age at first rape. The women seem to stand beneath a cascade of victimizations. But our victims are perpetrators as well. Having spent time in prison or jail is significantly correlated with the majority of the summary indicators (age at first rape once more being the exception), as is the case with the number of crimes the women committed as adults.[2]

Conclusions

The effects of violence on the lives of women in general have been well chronicled. Campbell and Lewandowski (1997) document both physical consequences (injury and death) and psychological consequences (primarily depression, but also post-traumatic stress disorder and other emotional disturbances). Another study concludes that clinically significant depression is nine times more common among abused and battered women than among women in general (Gleason 1993).

One would scarcely expect the effects of violence on the lives of homeless women to be any less severe, and indeed they are not. Virtually all of our measures of the frequency and severity of physical and sexual abuse as a child or an adult are significantly associated with negative life outcomes: physical injury, emotional devastation, loss of self-esteem, increased use of

---

2. The sequence of questions asks if respondents had ever shop-lifted, dealt drugs, driven while drunk, committed burglary or robbery, and so on (we asked about seventeen types of crime); if yes, how many times; and whether the women were arrested or convicted for any of the crimes. See chapter 3.

alcohol and drugs, and a variety of risky behaviors. Given all the enhanced stress that a lifetime of victimization brings, the remarkable thing about our data is that we did not find even more suicide attempts.

We conclude with some passages from Hayley's story. The daughter of alcoholic and abusive parents, she was molested by her brother at age two and was "having orgies" with the brother and his friends by age eight. She is schizophrenic, mutilates herself, abuses drugs, and has "been hurt by every single person I have ever met in life." Her occupational history includes ten years as a stripper, during which time she was "high on Ecstasy every single day." At age twenty-three, she won an amateur stripping contest, found out that her husband was "out smoking crack with some whores," and then tried to commit suicide: "I died for ten minutes, was brought back to life, then in a coma for three months." It was after the coma that she started stripping and using Ecstasy.

Hayley has a lifelong history of relationships with physically and sexually abusive men and has been in and out of a succession of shelters for battered women and the homeless. She has a son and a daughter, both of whom have also been sexually abused by her male companions. When asked how she felt about herself, she replied:

> I have no idea how to feel about myself. I have such an identity problem, it's not even funny. The person you see is not the person that I see . . . I don't even know who I am. I can't even look at myself in the mirror that much.

When we asked her to look back and reflect on her life as a whole, Hayley said:

> See, it's all the same. We create a cycle [that begins with child abuse]. Domestic violence is the after effect of child abuse, I believe. Drug addiction is the after effect of child abuse. Alcoholism is the after effect of child abuse. It all stems from when you're a child. Your parents make you what you are and then it's up to you to take it and go from there. And if all you are taught is bad, how do you do any good?

⹀ 10 ⹀

Conclusions

I think being homeless—as a homeless woman—is very degrading to
herself because you are already feeling bad about yourself and you don't
need nobody else to help you feel bad because you are already there. I think
a homeless woman, if she don't have to be homeless, should try her
darndest not to be homeless. —*Tamara*

Throughout this book, we have discussed how violence and homelessness
are inextricably linked. In fact, although the public perception is that homeless individuals are perpetrating violence, the reality is that they are much
more likely to be victims of violence (Donley 2008). The National Coalition
for the Homeless documents increasing attacks on homeless men, women,
and children, with the number of fatal attacks rising 40 percent from 2006
to 2007 (National Coalition for the Homeless 2009). Donley's (2008) analysis of the NSHAPC data demonstrates that nearly one in four homeless
individuals are physically assaulted or beaten up, and 7 percent are sexually
assaulted or raped while homeless. The NSHAPC data show that although
men and women are equally at risk for physical assault while homeless,
women are more than three times as likely as men to be victims of sexual
assault. This finding is consistent with the relationship between violence
and homelessness for women that has been our focus.

Indeed, the prevalence of sexual abuse in childhood and its later effects,
intimate partner victimization in adulthood, and heightened risks related
to sexual attack are all aspects to the relationship between violence and
homelessness for women that are uniquely gendered. Intimate partner victimization has been identified as a significant pathway toward homeless-

ness for women, and the National Alliance to End Homelessness has identified domestic violence as one of its important policy areas. With limited
affordable housing in general and long waiting lists for government-as-
sisted housing, women with few resources often are faced with the agoniz-
ing choice of staying with an abuser or becoming homeless. Current government and private resources are stretched to their limit and may not be
meeting the needs of everyone who is trying to escape domestic violence in
their home—and the need is enormous, as demonstrated by the annual
census of domestic violence services. On September 17, 2008, domestic
violence programs nationwide reported that more than 30,000 victims of
domestic violence received emergency shelter or transitional housing on
that day (National Network to End Domestic Violence 2008). This is the
number of women who were aware of resources and could find somewhere
to get help on one day. It excludes women who did not know where to turn
for help, felt they did not deserve help, or were prevented from seeking
help.

Our goal in this book has been to present a more complete picture than
what currently exists in the research of the complexities of homelessness
and violence for women. We did this through extensive surveying and in-
depth interviewing of more than 700 homeless women in Florida. We have
found violence to be a common thread connecting the life histories of these
women. It is part of the web of lived experiences that led each of them into
homelessness and that will challenge each of them throughout their lives.
Women like Tamara, one of the interview participants we quoted in earlier
chapters, have multiple experiences that illustrate how early victimization
shapes their identities and worldview. Consider Tamara's childhood. Her
abuse began when she was seven years old, when she was sexually victimized by her babysitter. This abuse continued for almost two years. As a
teenager, she was brutally raped by her sister's husband, who so damaged
her uterus that she was told she would be unable to bear children. In both
instances, family support was nonexistent, and Tamara had no support or
counseling to deal with her victimization:

So, but instead of dealing with my mental stability with those factors, they dealt
more with me not fitting in with the other children. I wasn't on the other children's level. And yeah, I did [become] withdrawn. I began to feel and act different. I wouldn't take baths with my sisters no more. I really didn't want to sleep

with them anymore, I didn't want to take off my clothes in front of them.
At school, I didn't want to play with anybody.

Tamara's experiences echo those of many of the women in our study. Abused as children, they has nobody to stand up for them and protect them. For Tamara, this was the beginning of a long journey of misdiagnoses, overmedication, and inattention:

They pronounced me back then as schizophrenic. And I've been labeled that for years. They put me on all kinds of medicines for that. One time, they put me on a medicine where I couldn't even get myself out of the chair. I couldn't function or focus off of the medicine so I stopped going to the mental health place and started going to Howard University mental health in Washington, D.C. and they did a test on me and found out that I'm not schizo. I suffer from post traumatic stress disorder with high depression. So all those years, they labeled me as having schizophrenia, and I never was.

Another result of Tamara's childhood abuse and its accompanying terror was low self-esteem. She says: "I remember the teacher in the classroom asking me questions. And like I'd be off somewhere else, looking out the window, because I knew at twelve o'clock Miss M [the abuser] was gonna come pick me up, so my head was never in school." School officials misinterpreted her marked social withdrawal as mental retardation, and Tamara was never adequately educated. Now fifty years old, she remains largely illiterate:

In special ed, they'll graduate you on a third grade level. They don't care. You go through the motions of cap and gown. Then they send you out there in the world on a second or third grade level. Thinking you're gonna go and get a job somewhere. What do you do if you can't read?

In adulthood, Tamara tried to educate herself. She started going to literacy classes and the library, wanting to fulfill her dream of attending college. After failed attempts to learn grammar in structured educational settings, she started hanging out in the park and talking to elderly individuals she met, with the goal of finding some way to make up for her lack of book learning. She says: "I can speak to someone and they won't look at me and say, 'Well, she's illiterate.' They look at me and say, 'Wow, that was a nice conversation.' And I developed that to hide the fact that I can't read or spell." The fact remains, however, that the educational system did not provide Tamara with even basic skills, which hindered her ability to survive, let alone thrive, as an independent adult.

Like many of the women in our study, the abuse that Tamara experienced during childhood was not limited to one type. In addition to sexual victimization, Tamara also endured physical violence from her stepfather. Her abusive baby sitter ensured Tamara's silence about her victimization by threatening her with her stepfather's abuse:

> My stepfather showed us love and then he showed us pain. What I mean by that, he would beat [us] with extension cords until our legs would bleed. But then he'd buy us anything and everything we needed . . . Miss M [the abusive baby sitter] knew that he beat us like that and she would always tell me that if I told [on her], my father was going to beat me.

Tamara also saw her stepfather regularly beat her mother. The combination of witnessing and experiencing violence clearly shaped her early social withdrawal. This withdrawal was accompanied by a retreat into an elaborate imaginary world:

> So basically, I lived in a world by myself. Even when I was younger being molested, I lived in a world by myself. I had my make-believe friends that I talked to, my friends that didn't hurt me. That I could trust. As I got older, like in junior high school, I still lived in a make-believe world. At the age of 15, 16, I still lived in a make-believe world. My world was kind, my world was sweet. I had my own characters within my world that I talked to. That was my safe place.

We highlight Tamara's childhood experiences here as illustrative of the lives of so many women in our study. Victimized and betrayed by their families, and ignored by societal institutions that could have interceded had they only paid more attention, these women did what they could to survive childhood. As we have shown, for many of the study participants, these events led to their early independence from their families, either as an escape or in an attempt to create better lives. Natalie, for example, left home at seventeen to marry her high-school sweetheart. Before that, her family made her feel "ugly and not loved." The man she started dating at fifteen was handsome and a little possessive. When they married two years later, the situation became abusive. Natalie says:

> He was good looking. He was constantly telling me that I was ugly, dumb, stupid. Couldn't do nothing right, the day that I got as fat as my mom he would divorce me. It was pretty violent at times. Black eyes, broken nose, broken ribs.

Similarly, Tamara's relationships with men in her twenties were abusive, with the boyfriends hitting, punching, and slapping her. She told us:

> I had to make a decision of who I am and what I want within my life. So I made a decision based on—all my life I have seen men beat women and I have more hatred towards that than I did with a woman . . . all my life seeing my father beat my mother with a belt, my sister's abusive husband that also raped and beat me. And then my boyfriends added to the—they're controlling, the cursing . . . I don't like the fact that they beat women and hurt women and they even kill women in the process of beating.

During her young adulthood, Tamara had a short career as a professional boxer. During this time she felt that she was living the good life, but things went downhill as she increasingly relied on cocaine and alcohol. She retired after six years and checked into a drug rehabilitation center. She went on to be a drug counselor, then a bus driver, and finally a maintenance worker. Earning an income enabled her to financially support her partner:

> With women, I think it started with Miss M. Miss M hurted [*sic*] me and when I started dealing with females, I wanted to be soft, I wanted to be gentle. I didn't want to hurt them. I wanted to be the opposite of Miss M. So basically in my relationships with women, I don't get hurt as far as physical. Mentally I do, because that's the way I am. I'd be abused. I'd be used. I'd give them my money. I'd buy them things. Always considerate and they would like me in the beginning, but then by me giving them all my money and things, they stopped liking me and they started to use me.

Indeed, Tamara chose as her romantic partners women who needed emotional and financial support: "I would always choose relationships that were bad, . . . the women who had low self-esteem like me or even lower. And by them having lower self-esteem than me, that gave me a little control or confidence within myself. Made myself feel a little good." Ultimately, her relationships with individuals who were needy or users drained her of resources, leading to her first episode of homelessness: "If they needed, I was there for them and it was like making up for Miss M, somewhere out there. So now I'm stuck three months behind [on rent], but I still had a job, but I couldn't catch up. I had nowhere to go. I didn't want to go to my family because of my pride. So, instead of going to them, I went to a shelter."

Again, Tamara's story illustrates how homelessness evolves in the lives of these women. Although she was working, her job did not pay enough to support her and her manipulative partner. Unwilling to ask for assistance from an abusive family, she went to a shelter, where violence once again played a role in her life: "In that shelter, you met all types of women. And they stole. They fought each other. You were scared to sleep at night. They would stab you. So I left." After lengthy stints on the streets, she was in a second shelter when we spoke with her. Like others in our study, Tamara came to Florida because of what the state seemed to promise: "the people were friendly and I said that one day I'm gonna move down here and I'll probably work for Walt Disney or Universal Studios." She called the homeless shelter in Orlando and asked how to secure a bed. Once she had a plan, Tamara moved to Orlando, got a bed in the shelter, and went looking for a job. Landing a job at a theme park, Tamara was scheduled to start not long after we spoke with her. She intended to remain at the shelter until she saved enough money to be on her own.

Violence in adulthood also permeated the women's experiences with homelessness, punctuating and extending it. In this book, we have discussed how homeless women endured more violence than the nonhomeless, with 75 percent of the women we surveyed having had something thrown at them; been pushed, grabbed, shoved, slapped, hit, kicked, bitten, shocked, beat up, or threatened with weapon; or had a weapon used against them. When the violence came from intimate partners, these abusers typically thwarted the women's attempts to keep a job or save money. Being homeless in itself also exposed the women to higher risks of violence on the street, which escalated related fears that were substantiated by their everyday experiences. The majority of homeless women in our study (55%) said they are "very concerned" about their physical safety and 21 percent say they carry something with them "to defend yourself or to alert other people" at least sometimes. More than a third of women told us that being a victim of violence had interfered with their ability to get or keep a job, and just over a quarter said this violence had interfered with their ability to find housing—both figures higher than comparable figures for the men we surveyed.

The women also perpetrated violence, typically after cumulative victimizations and sometimes as part of their strategy for survival. After enduring years of abuse from her husband, for example, Diane fought back:

> I busted beer bottles over his head. I did whatever I had to do to get him to understand, look this isn't happening anymore. I'm not gonna take this anymore. I'm either going to fight back—I'm gonna kill you, you're gonna kill me. Something is going to happen here. One of us is gonna end up dead.

Recall that nearly half the women in this study had spent time in prison or jail at some point in their adult lives, as had almost the entire sample of the men. Both these numbers are much higher than for the general U.S. population.

Limitations of our data aside, our study has taught us a great deal more about the experience of violence in the lives of homeless women than was known before. Among our most important findings are:

- Approximately one homeless woman in four is homeless mainly because of her experiences with violence. Although this percent is about half the frequently cited guess of one in two, it nonetheless underscores the importance of violence in the process by which some women become homeless.
- Homeless women are far more likely to experience violence of all sorts than American women in general—two to four times more likely, depending on the specific type of violence.
- Homeless men are more likely to experience violence of all sorts than American men in general.
- Homeless women are far more likely than homeless men to be victims of intimate partner violence.
- Homeless people of both genders are also frequent perpetrators of crime, although many of the crimes they commit are so-called survival crimes (such as stealing or prostitution) or somehow related to drug use.

- One reason why so many homeless women experience violence is that their routine daily activities expose them to potential offenders but do not provide them with capable guardians. The routines and sleeping patterns of homeless women are strongly related to high risks of victimization.
- By far the most significant risk factor for violent victimization as an adult is a pattern of physical, emotional, and sexual abuse as a child. Indeed, it is apparent in both the quantitative and qualitative components of our study that many of the young girls who became homeless adult women have been scarred by their childhood victimizations in ways that negatively affect their adult relationships.
- Victimized homeless women rarely report their victimizations to the authorities, and when they do, official responses are usually unsatisfactory.
- Establishing causal order in cross-sectional data is always tricky, but among the apparent consequences of violence in the lives of these women are increased substance abuse, emotional distress, and lowered self-esteem.

Our study clearly demonstrates that violence before, during, and after homelessness contributes to both its initiation and its perpetuation. Homeless women are a vulnerable population, with childhood violence at the crux of their vulnerability. At a minimum, these results suggest that more attention should be paid to the prevention and treatment of child victimization. Women in our study told us again and again how their childhood experiences negatively impacted their self-worth and other aspects of their self-concepts, their health, their ability to form relationships, and ultimately their ability to be independent and self-sufficient. Interactions with child service agencies consequently are an especially important intervention. Unfortunately, social services agencies including those charged with protecting the most vulnerable members of the population are woefully underfunded and understaffed, making it nearly impossible for them to create a safety net without holes. One important step toward stopping the cycle of abuse, therefore, is for child service agencies to receive adequate funding so they are able to provide necessary services. The women in our study also witnessed violence between their parents and other adults, but spoke little about any type of intervention for that type of violence. Coordinated responses from child protective workers and advocates for the victims of domestic violence could help fill the gap between needed services for both victims of domestic violence and their children.

From childhood on, their interactions with the criminal justice system and other services convinced the women in our study that agencies would rarely intervene for or protect them, either as victims of abuse or as homeless people. This lack of response was due in part to preconceived notions of the homeless as undeserving and somehow responsible for their victimization and homelessness. Though the original Violence Against Women Act and its revisions provided much-needed funds for law enforcement and judicial training, deeply rooted beliefs about violence against women remain. Before institutional changes can take place, attitudes must change so that such violence is no longer tolerated. Likewise, homeless individuals, often dehumanized in the media, are targets of violence and harassment. Indeed, some of the women in our study said that the police and the general public often seem to view homelessness itself as a criminal condition. Changing some of these attitudes is a necessary early step.

The women in our study were at that time homeless and in a shelter. Homeless shelters, by necessity, focus on the most pressing needs—typically bed and board—and are not always equipped to handle the myriad problems that homeless women bring with them. Further, many shelters do not provide a sufficiently secure and stable environment to promote good child development for children from violent homes. Wright, Rubin, and Devine find that "street homeless and sheltered homeless are not distinct populations; nearly all the homeless people in this sample spent at least an occasional night in an emergency shelter and nearly all of them also occasionally slept out of doors. Which homeless people are considered 'sheltered homeless' depends a great deal on who makes it to the shelter line first" (1998, 61). Clearly, homeless shelters are not the ideal solution and serve only as a temporary haven for some homeless individuals. Until more affordable housing is available, however, shelters are the only housing option for many people. Our study clearly indicates that even prior to the women's arrival at a shelter, however, there are multiple points at which social institutions could have interceded, possibly preventing the types of repetitive violence that these women experienced and keeping them from becoming homeless. Educational institutions, child welfare services, and law enforcement agencies all had extensive contact with the majority of the women in our study, yet none successfully changed the direction of these women's lives for the better.

What can be done when not just one agency but entire networks of systems somehow miss so many girls and women falling through the cracks? This failure points to a larger ideological paradigm that reinforces existing inequalities while ignoring their impact on at-risk and marginalized segments of the population. Attitudes of indifference and blame toward victims of violence and the homeless pervade not only the agencies designed to protect these groups, but affect the political agendas and funding opportunities that could address glaring deficiencies in how we meet the groups' needs.

In recent years, homelessness has faded from prominence as a national political issue. However, there seems to be a widespread sense among both policymakers and the public that what we tried to do in the 1980s was hopelessly insufficient. While the increasing number of homeless women and children is acknowledged by almost everybody, no one seems to know why this is the case, or how to prevent it. We have seen that homelessness among women is intimately linked to the violence they experience as children and adults, so the path to prevention is to stop the violence perpetrated against them. Understanding the impact of violence on housing is also paramount. Women leaving abusive relationships are faced with the harsh reality that their abuser has isolated them and is attempting to sabotage their efforts toward financial independence. Consequently, these women often lack support networks of family and friends and are forced to rely on what limited social services are available. Providing more and greater access to resources (including affordable housing) may be one mechanism for increasing the options for women attempting to escape from violent relationships. Further, as we have seen, many of the processes that put women out on the streets are gendered, ranging from the sorts of victimizations they experience in early childhood to the survival options available to young girls on the streets. As Bob Herbert noted in *The New York Times*: "we have become so accustomed to living in a society saturated with misogyny that the barbaric treatment of women and girls has come to be more or less expected" (Herbert 2009). For the women in our study, violence was a part of their everyday existence, as had been their constant struggle to keep a roof over their head. As Tamara says: "Who cares, you know? Who fights for the homeless people? Who cares?"

The fact that many homeless women are homeless and remain home-less because of violence is an indication of where we need to focus our at-tention, efforts, and resources. In times of economic downturn, emergency crisis responses often siphon funding away from prevention efforts. At the same time, the need for these efforts increases. Without efforts to stop vio-lence in the home, generation after generation of children will grow up in unstable, often unsafe, households and consequently be at an increased risk of repeating the cycle of violence and becoming homeless. Coordinated community responses that include prevention messages alongside inter-ventions have the potential to reduce the number of women who face both violent victimization and homelessness. If we work to reduce violence, questions like Tamara's will no longer have to be asked.

Appendix A

Study Methodology

The Florida Four-City Study of Violence in the Lives of Homeless Women was designed to be a multisite, statewide study. As indicated in the text, the literature on violence and homeless women tends to be dominated by single-city or even single-shelter (or single-facility) surveys. We felt that it was important to obtain data from multiple sites in order to avoid overgeneralizing results that might be unique to a particular site. In general, differences across the four cities in the study were substantively minor and statistically not significant, with a few important exceptions discussed later in this appendix. So we may be reasonably confident that our findings generalize at least to urban homeless women in Florida, if not to homeless women everywhere in the United States.

Initial Focus Group

Altogether, over 700 homeless women participated in the study, development of which began with a focus group in November 2002 at an Orlando domestic violence shelter. This initial focus group involved six women who were part of an outpatient group of domestic violence survivors who had also experienced homelessness. The purpose of this focus group was to pinpoint the key issues relevant to homeless women and their experiences with violence, and to make sure that the larger study not only reflected the topics that had surfaced in our review of the scientific literature, but that it adequately reflected the life stories of the women we intended to study. Many themes and perspectives emerged from this initial focus group and were used over the next several months to develop a survey questionnaire.

The Survey

The survey questionnaire was designed to be administered by interviewers at each of the four sites across Florida (Orlando, Tampa, Jacksonville, and Miami, the four largest metropolitan areas in the state). Interviewer training in each of the four sites commenced shortly after the questionnaire was completed, and as soon as training was completed, interviewing began. Interviewers in each site were recruited from among existing shelter staff—mostly case managers, intake workers, and counselors. All our interviewers were highly experienced in dealing with homeless women and their problems, and all took on their interviewing jobs as a supplement to their normal work roles. Our interviewers dealt with issues of violence and victimization on a daily basis. They were already screened, trained, and provided with resources to deal with any adverse personal reactions that respondents might have in the course of the interview. In fact, although some women had strong emotional reactions during the interview (hardly a surprise, given the subject matter), none of these reactions was strong enough to require professional intervention or to rise to the level of an adverse event that had to be reported to an institutional review board.

Interviewers were given advice during training about how to deal with respondents' signs of emotion or discomfort, including allowing the interviewee to take breaks, demonstrating empathy, discontinuing the interview, and so on. We also reinforced the point that if the interview produced any sign of renewed victimization or traumatization, the interviewee must be referred to the appropriate clinical staff person at the shelter. However, to our knowledge, no such signs occurred. As part of the training, interviewers were instructed to record nonverbal cues in the margins of the survey instrument. These cues were used as a way to help the interviewer determine whether to probe further, and how to assess the interviewee's level of discomfort, reluctance, or other emotional issues.

Interviewers were trained to conduct their normal intake process, and during intake to ask the client if she was willing to participate in a study conducted by faculty at the University of Central Florida and funded by the National Institute of Justice. The purpose of the interview, clients were told, was to gain insight and understanding into the lives of women who were experiencing homelessness. Prospective participants were also told that they had been chosen at random. All participants signed a consent form that outlined the purpose and goals of the study. In addition, they were given a copy of this form in case they wanted to refer to it later. The form contained contact information for the study director, so that participants with questions could call him.

All aspects of the study protocol, including the consent forms, survey questionnaire, guiding questions for the focus group, and the protocols for the in-depth personal interviews, were reviewed and approved by the institutional review board of the University of Central Florida. Copies of the consent forms and questionnaires are available from the authors on request (send an email inquiry to jjasinsk@mail.ucf.edu).

The survey sample was comprised of about 200 face-to-face interviews with homeless women in each of four Florida cities. Altogether, 737 women were interviewed. In Orlando, 199 women were interviewed at the Coalition for the Homeless of Central Florida. In Tampa, 200 women were interviewed at the Metropolitan Ministries facilities. In Jacksonville, 146 women were interviewed at the I.M. Sulz-bacher Center for the Homeless. In Miami, 192 women were interviewed at the Community Partnership for the Homeless, Inc. These four facilities made our study possible, and we are pleased to acknowledge our gratitude to each of them. The sample of homeless women was supplemented with a sample of about 100 homeless men recruited at The Men's Pavilion, the men's facility of the Orlando Coalition for the Homeless. All the women chosen for in-depth qualitative inter-views were also from the Orlando facility, because this was more convenient than trying to identify and interview women all over the state.

Qualitative Interviews

In-depth qualitative interviews were conducted in Orlando with 20 homeless women who had also been victims of violence. All these women were staying at one of two homeless centers in Orlando, both of them affiliated with the Coalition for the Homeless of Central Florida. Access to the women at these two shelters was facili-tated by community contacts that we had already established, since one of us (Wright) sits on the board of directors for the Coalition for the Homeless of Central Florida. Women who took part in the qualitative study were recruited by case man-agers who had also participated in our survey interview training. They were asked to identify women at the centers who had experienced some form of violence. The first twenty women who fit this criterion and agreed to be interviewed were the participants for the qualitative study. Such purposive sampling (Babbie 1995) was appropriate since in qualitative research, interviewees are often intentionally cho-sen for the specific perspectives and life experiences they may have (Esterberg 2002).

In-depth interviews took place between September 2003 and January 2004 and were arranged by the case managers, who would set up mutually convenient meet-ings between one of us (Wesely) and the participant in a private conference or sitting room at the homeless center. Averaging two hours, the interviews were audiotaped, then transcribed and coded. Pseudonyms are used throughout this manuscript to protect the identities of the respondents. Their ages at the time of the interviews ranged from nineteen to sixty-two years, with an average age of forty.

The qualitative interviews were exploratory and were intended to add richness and depth by focusing on the narratives of the women. By documenting the lives of the women we interviewed, exploring the experiences of the women from their own point of view, and understanding their choices and actions within a larger social context (Reinharz 1992), another dimension was added to the findings that emerged from the survey research. Results from these qualitative interviews are woven throughout the text of this book and are used whenever possible to enrich, deepen, explain, or expand upon the more quantitative survey results.

Survey Sampling

To select women for the study, we entered into a cooperative agreement with a large, general-purpose shelter for the homeless in each of the four cities. Each of the four facilities provides shelter and other services to hundreds of homeless people daily, both men and women. All of the shelters where respondents were solicited are general-purpose homeless facilities, not battered women's facilities (which would amount to sampling on the dependent variable) and not facilities devoted exclusively to such groups as teens, the addicted, women, or the mentally ill (which could have introduced possible biases).

Our initial plan was to interview the first 200 women who came through the doors of our participating facilities during the data collection period. Recognizing the logistical difficulties of implementing any specific sampling plan in a social service context often characterized by crisis and relative chaos, we allowed for some deviation from this desideratum. During interviewer training, however, we stressed the need to avoid interviewing only those women who somehow looked like victims of violence, or those who indicated in an intake interview that they had had recent problems with violence. All our interviewers seemed to understand this point and its importance to the goals of the survey.

Survey Contents

One reason why the literature on violence and homeless women contains a hodgepodge of results is the general avoidance of standardized, validated measuring instruments in favor of various ad hoc measures that are unique to each study. Our strategy was to use standardized instruments wherever possible, modified as necessary and appropriate given our population and hypotheses.

The Conflict Tactics Scale (Straus 1979), as modified by Tjaden and Thoennes (1998, 1999), was used to measure the occurrence of "major violence" episodes among homeless women. The modifications of the scale by Tjaden and Thoennes make it equally useful in measuring violence committed by intimates or strangers (i.e., both domestic and street violence perpetrated against these women). The modified scale also asks about violence experienced both as a child and as an adult, inquires about the consequences of victimization, and records details on the reporting of violent experiences, and what happened after reporting. In essence, these modifications transform the scale into a survey instrument similar to that used in the National Victimization Surveys. These modifications not only make the scale more useful in investigating violence against homeless women but also allow comparisons to a national sample of women (Tjaden and Thoennes 1998). The Conflict Tactics Scale has demonstrated reliability and validity.

The Personal History Form (PHF) is a standardized instrument widely used in studies of homeless people to record family and background characteristics, housing and homelessness histories, recent residential information, lifetime homeless episodes, most recent homeless episode, and the like. We gained extensive experience with the PHF in the New Orleans Homeless Substance Abusers Project (see Wright, Devine, and Joyner 1993 for a copy of the instrument). The only significant modifications required for the purposes of the present study, other than the deletion of some irrelevant items, were (1) to substitute the Tjaden-Thoennes childhood abuse sequence for the one contained in the PHF (the former is far more detailed and informative) and (2) to expand the allowable responses to the questions about "the reasons people have for leaving their residences" (in all the sequences about why the respondent is homeless) to specifically include intimate partner violence as one possible reason.

The Addiction Severity Index (ASI; McLellan et al. 1992) is a widely used instrument that obtains detailed information on the respondent's medical status, employment and financial support, drug and alcohol use, legal status, family history and conflict, and psychiatric status. Again, we have extensive experience administering the ASI and have published on its methodological properties in research on homeless substance abusers (Joyner, Wright, and Devine 1996). Much of the ASI repeats items from the PHF and the modified Conflict Tactics Scale; redundant items were eliminated. Also, not all sections of the ASI are equally relevant to the aims of this study. From the legal status sequence, for example, our only interest was in the items asking about prior convictions (to test the hypothesis that homeless women with criminal records experience more violence than those without). Very little from the medical status sequence was retained; moreover, most of the items in the section on employment and support that deal with survival strategies needed to be supplemented with additional items. Please note: the modifications we made to the ASI make it impossible to compute so-called ASI scores for respondents in our survey.)

Qualitative Interview Contents

The qualitative in-depth interviews were semistructured and based on a set of open-ended, guiding questions that corresponded to general topical areas. Semistructured, in-depth interviews are "particularly useful in gathering information about stigmatized, uncomfortable, or difficult areas in subjects' lives" (Richie 1996, 16). The topic areas addressed in this study included background and childhood, family relationships both as a child and as an adult, intimate relationships, power and control, violence, abuse, and homelessness. One of us (Wesely, who conducted the interviews) remained open throughout the process to emerging patterns that might suggest additional questions and probes to be incorporated.

A two-stage process of coding was utilized. First, open coding (Esterberg 2002) allowed us to identify the themes and patterns that emerged in the transcripts of the interviews. As themes became evident, we focused on the organization of these themes. During this second phase, focused coding (Esterberg 2002), we revisited the transcripts line by line to solidify central categories as well as accompanying subthemes. Subthemes were identified as those that supported or explicated the more general themes that emerged. During analysis, we remained open to discon-firming evidence, or cases that did not support the themes we identified.

Differences across Cities

A second possible reason for the generally chaotic state of the literature on the ex-perience of violence by homeless women is that almost all extant studies are single-site studies, and it is likely that the true underlying rate of violence (against people in general, against women, and against homeless women) varies from one site or city to the next. Our study was done in four cities in order to explore this hypothesis. Unfortunately, since the data were collected in only one facility per city, facility differences and city differences are fatally confounded in the data. Thus, in the text we present only the combined data for all four cities and treat the sample as repre-sentative of urban homeless women in Florida.

That said, there were some predictable differences across the four city samples that readers need to be aware of. Miami, for example, had the highest percentages of Hispanic and African American women; Orlando and Jacksonville had the high-est percentages of whites. Miami women were more likely to have never married; Tampa women, most likely to have borne a child.

Homeless histories also varied across cities, but within a fairly narrow range. Women's average age when first becoming homeless varied from thirty to thirty-six years and averaged thirty-three years; average total years homeless varied from 1.0 years (Jacksonville) to 2.3 years (Tampa); the percentage homeless by themselves (that is, not with a partner, with children, or both) ranged from 40.0 percent to 61.3 percent.

We asked each of the women if they were currently homeless because of violence or abuse committed against them by an adult partner in their last residence. About three-quarters of the women in all four cities told us that violence was not a factor in their current episode of homelessness.

Although large proportions of the women in all four cities identified themselves as victims of violence, there were large and significant city differences in the overall victimization rates. Women in Tampa were the most likely to report any sexual or physical victimization (89.5%), and women in Miami were the least likely (64.1%). Women from Orlando (79.4%) and Jacksonville (76.0%) were in between. Unfortunately, these differences do not exactly mirror the rates of violent crime in the four cities (which would otherwise be an obvious explanation). Tampa has the highest violent crime rate, and women from Tampa were indeed the most likely to be victims. On the other hand, Jacksonville has the least amount of crime, but Jacksonville women did not report the least victimization—that distinction goes to women from Miami. This pattern suggests that the victimization experiences of homeless women do not depend entirely on their city of residence, but that city-specific effects may be important.

We also examined the city differences in multivariate models, holding various demographic and homeless background characteristics common. The multivariate results suggest that some demographic factors are protective (decreasing the risk for adult victimization), while others act as risk factors (increasing the risk). Being divorced or separated (as opposed to being married), being homeless more often, and having more children were associated with increased odds of victimization as an adult. In contrast, African American and Hispanic women (compared to white women) were less likely to be victimized. Finally, net of all other variables in the model, women from Miami were still less likely to be victims, for reasons that we cannot pretend to understand.

It is, of course, possible that our Miami respondents differed from other respondents in factors that we have not measured or have not included in the analysis. The residual effect for living in Miami, that is, may still be spurious. But it might also be real, and if it is, then the implication is that homeless women in different cities may experience violence at significantly different rates. This is not a surprising result per se. Serious students of crime would be far more surprised to learn that all homeless women suffered equivalent levels of victimization, regardless of city context. The importance of the finding lies only in the implication for how we interpret victimization results from single-site studies, or how we can compare different results as reported from different cities. The possibility of real differences in victimization rates across cities apparently undermines the value of single-site studies and findings. On the other hand, we observed many fewer significant differences across our four Florida cities than we anticipated, so perhaps the more prudent conclusion is that, at least in most cases, the common material and existential conditions of homelessness tend to overwhelm other city-level factors.

Appendix B

Serious Physical Abuse Items

Childhood Serious Physical Abuse

When you were a child, did any parent, step parent, guardian, or other person:

Push, shove, or grab you?
Hit you with an object?
Slap your face?
Kick you or hit you with a fist?
Threaten you with a knife or gun?
Burn or scald you on purpose?
Cut you?
Threaten to kill you?
Use a knife or gun on you?
Choke you?
Neglect you?
Beat you up?

Adult Serious Physical Abuse

Since you became an adult did, any person, male or female, ever:

Slap or hit you?
Kick or bite you?
Choke or attempt to drown you?
Hit you with an object?
Beat you up?
Threaten you with a gun?
Threaten you with a knife or some other weapon besides a gun?
Use a gun on you?
Use a knife or some other weapon on you?

References

Alexander, Mary J. 1996. Women with co-occurring addictive and mental disorders: An emerging profile of vulnerability. *American Journal of Orthopsychiatry* 66:61–70.

Arnold, Regina A. 1990. Women of color: Processes of victimization and criminalization of black women. *Social Justice* 173:153–66.

Avakame, Edem F., and James J. Fyfe, 2001. Differential police treatment of male-on-female spousal violence: Additional evidence on the leniency thesis. *Violence against Women* 7:22–45.

Babbie, Earl. 1995. *The Practice of Social Research.* 7th ed. Belmont, CA: Wadsworth.

Baker, Charlene K., Sarah L. Cook, and Fran N. Norris. 2003. Domestic violence and housing problems: A contextual analysis of women's help-seeking, received informal support, and formal system response. *Violence against Women* 9:754–83.

Bartky, Sandra. 1990. *Femininity and Domination.* New York: Routledge.

Barnett, Ola, Miller-Perrin, Cindy L., and Robin Perrin. 2005. *Family Violence across the Lifespan: An Introduction.* 2nd ed. Thousand Oaks, CA: Sage.

Belknap, Joanne. 2007. *The Invisible Woman: Gender, Crime and Justice.* 3rd ed. Belmont, CA: Thomson Wadsworth.

Belknap, Joanne, D. L. R. Graham, P. G. Allen, J. Hartman, V. Lippen, and J. Sutherland. 1999. Predicting court outcomes in intimate partner violence cases: Preliminary findings. *Domestic Violence Report* 5:9–10.

Belknap, Joanne, and Kristi Holsinger. 1998. An overview of delinquent girls: How theory and practice have failed and the need for innovative change. In *Female Offenders: Critical Perspectives and Effective Interventions*, edited by Ruth T. Zaplin, 31–64. Gaithersburg, MD: Aspen.

Bennett, Larry. 1995. Substance abuse and the domestic assault of women. *Social Work* 40:760–71.

Bonczar, Thomas P. 2003. *Prevalence of Imprisonment in the U.S. Population, 1974–2001.* Washington: U.S. Department of Justice, Bureau of Justice Statistics.

Bordo, Susan. 1993. *Unbearable Weight.* Berkeley: University of California Press.

Breton, Margot, and Terry Bunston. 1992. Physical and sexual violence in the lives of homeless women. *Canadian Journal of Community Mental Health* 11:29–44.

Brett, Crista. 1993. From victim to victimizer. In *Female Offenders: Meeting the Needs of a Neglected Population*, 26–30. Laurel, MD: American Correctional Association.

Brickner, Phillip W., Lina K. Scharer, Barbara A. Conanan, Marianne Savarese, and Brian C. Sealnan, eds. 1990. *Under the Safety Net: The Health and Social Welfare of the Homeless in the United States*. New York: W. W. Norton.

Brinegar, Sarah J. 2003. The social construction of homeless shelters in the Phoenix area. *Urban Geography* 24:61–74.

Browne, Angela. 1993. Family violence and homelessness: The relevance of trauma histories in the lives of homeless women. *American Journal of Orthopsychiatry* 63:370–84.

——— and Shari Bassuk. 1997. Intimate violence in the lives of homeless and poor housed women: Prevalence and patterns in an ethnically diverse sample. *American Journal of Orthopsychiatry* 67:261–78.

Browne, Angela, Amy Salomon, and Shari Bassuk. 1999. The impact of recent partner violence on poor women's capacity to maintain work. *Violence against Women* 5:393–426.

Bufkin, Jana L., and Judith Bray. 1998. Domestic violence, criminal justice responses, and homelessness: Finding the connection and addressing the problem. *Journal of Social Distress and the Homeless* 7:227–40.

Burt, Martha, Laudan Y. Aron, and Edgar Lee. 2001. *Helping America's Homeless: Emergency Shelter or Affordable Housing?* Washington: Urban Institute Press.

Buzawa, Carl G., and Thomas L. Austin. 1993. Determining police response to domestic violence victims. *American Behavioral Scientist* 36:610–23.

Buzawa, Eve S., and Carl G. Buzawa. 2003. *Domestic Violence: The Criminal Justice Response*. 3rd ed. Thousand Oaks, CA: Sage.

Campbell, Jacquelyn C., and Linda A. Lewandowski. 1997. Mental and physical health effects of intimate partner violence on women and children. *Psychiatric Clinics of North America* 20:353–74.

Carey-Webb, Allen. 1992. Representing the homeless. *American Literary History* 4: 697–708.

Catalano, Shannan M. 2004. *Criminal Victimization, 2003*. U.S. Department of Justice, Office of Justice Programs. http://www.ojp.usdoj.gov/bjs/pub/pdf/cv03.pdf (accessed September 5, 2009).

Catalano, Shannan M. 2006. *Criminal Victimization, 2005*. Washington: U.S. Department of Justice, Office of Justice Programs. http://www.ojp.usdoj.gov/bjs/pub/pdf/cv05.pdf (accessed September 15, 2009).

Centers for Disease Control. 2005. QuickStats: Average age of mothers at first birth, by state—United States, 2002. *Morbidity and Mortality Weekly Report* 54, May

19–20, http://www.cdc.gov/mmwr/PDF/wk/mm5419.pdf (accessed September 23, 2009).

Chapkis, Wendy. 1986. *Beauty Secrets: Women and the Politics of Appearance*. Boston: South End.

Charles, Nickie. 1994. Domestic violence, homelessness and housing: The response of housing providers in Wales. *Critical Social Policy* 14:36–52.

Chesney-Lind, Meda, and Lisa Pasko. 2004. *The Female Offender: Girls, Women and Crime*. 2nd ed. Thousand Oaks, CA: Sage.

Chesney-Lind, Meda, and Noelie Rodriguez. 1983. Women under lock and key. *Prison Journal* 63:47–65.

Clarke, Pamela, Nancy C. Pendry, and Yeoun S. Kim. 1997. Patterns of violence in homeless women. *Western Journal of Nursing Research* 19:490–500.

Cohen, Lawrence E., and Marcus Felson. 1979. Social change and crime rate trends: A routine activity approach. *American Sociological Review* 44:588–608.

Conaway, Mark R., and Sharon L. Lohr. 1994. A longitudinal analysis of factors associated with reporting violent crimes to the police. *Journal of Quantitative Criminology* 10:23–39.

Culhane, Dennis P., Edmund F. Dejowski, Julie Ibanez, Elizabeth Needham, and Irene Macchia. 1994. Public shelter admission rates in Philadelphia and New York City: The implications of turnover for sheltered population counts. *Housing Policy Debate* 52:107–39.

Culhane, Dennis P., and Randall Kuhn. 1997. Patterns and determinants of shelter utilization among single homeless adults in New York City and Philadelphia: A longitudinal analysis of homelessness. *Journal of Policy Analysis and Management* 171:23–43.

Culhane, Dennis P., and Stephen Metraux. 1999. One-year prevalence rates of public shelter utilization by race, sex, age and poverty status for New York City 1990, 1995 and Philadelphia 1995. *Population Research and Policy Review* 183:219–36.

Daley, Kathleen, and Meda Chesney-Lind. 1988. Feminism and criminology. *Justice Quarterly* 5:497–538.

Dasgupta, Shamita Das. 2001. *Towards an Understanding of Women's Use of Nonlethal Violence in Intimate Heterosexual Relationships*. National Online Resource Center on Violence Against Women, http://new.vawnet.org/Assoc_Files_VAW net/AR_womviol.pdf (accessed September 15, 2009).

Davis, PhillipW. 1983. Restoring the semblance of order: Police strategies in the domestic disturbance. *Symbolic Interaction* 6:261–78.

De Simone, Peter, Tom Gould, and John J. Stretch. 1998. *Homelessness in Missouri: Eye of the Storm?* Jefferson City, MO: Missouri Association for Social Welfare.

DeKeseredy, Walter S., and Martin D. Schwartz. 2009. *Dangerous Exits: Escaping Abusive Relationships in Rural America*. New Brunswick, NJ: Rutgers University Press.

DeLisi, Matt. 2000. Who is more dangerous? Comparing the criminality of adult homeless and domiciled jail inmates: A research note. *International Journal of Offender Therapy and Comparative Criminology* 441:59–69.

Dennis, Deborah L., Irene S. Levine, and Fred C. Osher. 1991. The physical and mental health status of homeless adults. *Housing Policy Debate* 2:815–35.

D'Ercole, Ann, and Elmer Struening. 1990. Victimization among homeless women: Implications for service delivery. *Journal of Community Psychology* 18:141–52.

Dobash, Rebecca E., and Russell P. Dobash. 1979. *Violence against Wives: A Case against the Patriarchy*. New York: Free Press.

———. 1992. *Women, Violence and Social Change*. London: Routledge.

———. 1998. *Rethinking Violence against Women*. Thousand Oaks, CA: Sage.

Donley, Amy. 2008. The perception of homeless people: Important factors in determining perceptions of the homeless as dangerous. Ph.D. diss., University of Central Florida.

Dotson, Hilary. 2009. Homeless women in the Orlando shelter system: A comparison of single women, families, and women separated from their children. Master's thesis, University of Central Florida.

Duffy, John C., and Jennifer J. Waterto. 2006. Under-reporting of alcohol consumption in sample surveys. *Addiction* 79:303–8.

Eigenberg, Helen. 2001. *Woman Battering in the United States: Till Death Do Us Part*. Prospect Heights, IL: Waveland.

Erez, Edna, and Joanne Belknap. 1998. In their own words: Battered women's assessment of the criminal processing system's response. *Violence and Victims* 13: 251–68.

Esterberg, Kristin. 2002. *Qualitative Methods in Social Research*. Boston: McGraw-Hill.

Feder, Lynette. 1998. Police handling of domestic and nondomestic assault calls: Is there a case for discrimination? *Crime and Delinquency* 44:335–89.

Felson, Richard B., and Jeff Ackerman. 2001. Arrest for domestic and other assaults. *Criminology* 39:655–76.

Ferraro, Kathleen J. 2006. *Neither Angels nor Demons: Women, Crime, and Victimization*. Hanover, NH: University Press of New England.

Ferraro, Kenneth F. 1995. *Fear of Crime: Interpreting Victimization Risk*. Albany: State University of New York Press.

Fischer, Pamela J., Alan Ross, and William R. Breakey. 1993. Correlates of arrest in a Baltimore homeless population. *Contemporary Drug Problems* 20, no. 3:385–414.

Fisher, Barbara, Mel Hovell, C. Richard Hofstetter, and Richard Hough. 1995. Risks associated with long-term homelessness among women: Battery, rape and HIV infection. *International Journal of Health Services* 25:351–69.

Fyfe, James J., David A. Klinger, and Jeanne M. Flavin. 1997. Differential police treatment of male-on-female spousal violence. *Criminology* 35:455–73.

Gaarder, Emily, and Joanne Belknap. 2002. Tenuous borders: Girls transferred to adult court. *Criminology* 40:481–517.

Gans, Herbert J. 1995. *The War against the Poor: The Underclass and Anti-poverty Policy.* New York: Basic.

Gardner, Carol B. 1995. *Passing By: Gender and Public Harassment.* Berkeley: University of California Press.

Gartner, Rosemary I., and Ross I. Macmillan. 1995. The effect of victim-offender relationship on police knowledge of incidents of violence against women. *Canadian Journal of Criminology* 37:393–430.

Geissler, Lisal J., Carol A. Bormann, Carol F. Kwiatkowski, G. Nicholas Braucht, and Charles S. Reichardt. 1995. Women, homelessness, and substance abuse: Moving beyond the stereotypes. *Psychology of Women Quarterly* 19:65–83.

Gilbert, Louisa, Nabila El-Bassel, Robert F. Schilling, and Ellen Friedman. 1997. Childhood abuse as a risk factor for partner abuse among women in methadone maintenance. *American Journal of Drug and Alcohol Abuse* 23:581–95.

Giles-Sims, Jean. 1998. The aftermath of partner violence. In *Partner Violence: A Comprehensive Review of 20 Years of Research,* edited by Jana L. Jasinski and Linda M. Williams, 44–72. Thousand Oaks, CA: Sage.

Gilfus, Mary E. 1992. From victims to survivors to offenders: Women's routes of entry and immersion into street crime. *Women and Criminal Justice* 4:63–90.

———. 2006. From victims to survivors to offenders: Women's routes of entry and immersion into street crime. In *In Her Own Words: Women Offenders' Views on Crime and Incarceration,* edited by Leanne F. Alarid and Paul Cromwell, 5–14. Los Angeles: Roxbury.

Gleason, Walter J. 1993. Mental disorders in battered women: An empirical study. *Violence and Victims* 8:53–68

Goodman, Lisa A. 1991. The prevalence of abuse in the lives of homeless and housed poor mothers: A comparison study. *American Journal of Orthopsychiatry* 61:489–500.

——— and Mary Ann Dutton. 1996. The impact of victimization on cognitive schemata among homeless, seriously mentally ill women. *Violence and Victims* 11: 159–74.

——— and Maxine Harris. 1995. Episodically homeless women with serious mental illness: Prevalence of physical and sexual assault. *American Journal of Orthopsychiatry* 65:468–78.

———. 1997. The relationship between violence dimensions and symptom severity among homeless mentally ill women. *Journal of Traumatic Stress* 10:51–70.

Greenan, Lily. 2004. *Violence against Women: A Literature Review.* Edinburgh: Blackwell.

Griffin, Susan. 1981. *Pornography and Silence.* New York: Harper and Row.

Hagan, John, and Bill McCarthy. 1997. *Mean Streets: Youth Crime and Homelessness.* Cambridge: Cambridge University Press.

Herbert, Bob. 2009. Women at risk. *The New York Times*, August 7.

Herman, Judith. 1997. *Trauma and Recovery.* New York: Basic.

Hilfiker, David. 1989. Are we comfortable with homelessness? *Journal of the American Medical Association* 262:1375–76.

Hindelang, Michael J., Michael R. Gottfreson, and James Garofalo. 1978. *Victims of Personal Crime: An Empirical Foundation for a Theory of Personal Victimization.* Cambridge, MA: Ballinger.

Hirsch, Kathleen. 1989. *Songs from the Alley.* New York: Ticknor and Fields.

Hofford, Meredith, and Adele V. Harrell. 1993. *Family Violence: Interventions for the Justice System.* Washington: U.S. Department of Justice, Bureau of Justice Assistance.

Hollander, Jocelyn A. 2001. Vulnerability and dangerousness: The construction of gender through conversations about violence. *Gender and Society* 15:83–109.

Homes for the Homeless. 1998. *A Snapshot of Family Homelessness across America: Ten Cities, 1997–1998.* New York: Institute for Children and Poverty.

Hopper, Kim. 2003. *Reckoning with Homelessness.* Ithaca, NY: Cornell University Press.

Hwang, Stephen W. 2001. Homelessness and health. *Canadian Medical Association Journal* 164, no. 2. http://www.cmaj.ca/cgi/content/full/164/2/229 (accessed on March 23, 2009).

Hynes, H. Patricia, and Janice G. Raymond. 2002. Put in harm's way: The neglected health consequences of sex trafficking in the United States. In *Policing the National Body: Sex, Race, and Criminalization*, edited by J. Silliman and A. Bhattacharjee, 197–229. Cambridge, MA: South End.

Ingram, Kathleen M., Alexandra F. Corning, and Lyle D. Schmidt. 1996. The relationship of victimization experiences to psychological well-being among homeless women and low-income housed women. *Journal of Counseling Psychology* 43:218–27.

Institute of Medicine Committee on Health Care for Homeless People. 1988. *Homelessness, Health and Human Needs.* Washington: National Academy Press.

James, Doris. 2004. *Profile of Jail Inmates, 2002.* Washington: U.S. Department of Justice, Bureau of Justice Statistics.

James, Jennifer, and Jane Meyerding. 1977. Early sexual experience as a factor in prostitution. *Archives of Sexual Behavior* 7:31–42.

Janus, Mark D., Ann W. Burgess, Carol R. Hartman, and Arlene McCormack. 1987. *Adolescent Runaways: Causes and Consequences.* Lexington, MA: Lexington.

Jensen, Gary F., and David Brownfield. 1986. Gender, lifestyles and victimization: Beyond routine activity. *Violence and Victims* 12:85–99.

Johnson, Michael P. 2001. Conflict and control: Images of symmetry and asymmetry in domestic violence. In *Couples in Conflict*, edited by A. Booth, A. C. Crouter, and M. Clements, 95–104. Hillsdale, NJ: Erlbaum.

———. 2008. *A Typology of Domestic Violence: Intimate Terrorism, Violent Resistance, and Situational Couple Violence.* Hanover, NH: Northeastern University Press.

Joyner, Laurie, James D. Wright, and Joel Devine. 1996. Reliability and validity of the Addiction Severity Index among homeless substance misusers. *Substance Use and Misuse* 31:729–51.

Kannah, Mukti, Nirbhay N. Singh, Mary Nemil, Al Best, and Cynthia R. Ellis. 1992. Homeless women and their families: Characteristics, life circumstances, and needs. *Journal of Child and Family Studies* 1:155–65.

Kaufman Kantor, Glenda, and Jana L. Jasinski. 1998. Dynamics and risk factors in partner violence. In *Partner Violence: A Comprehensive Review of 20 Years of Research*, edited by Jana L. Jasinski and Linda M. Williams, 1–43. Thousand Oaks, CA: Sage.

Kershner, Marilyn K. 2003. *When There's Nowhere to Go: Domestic Violence and the Need for Better Housing Options for Survivors and Their Children.* Tampa, FL: Children's Board of Hillsborough County.

Kilpatrick, Dean G., Ronald Acierno, Heidi Resnick, Benjamin Saunders, and Connie L. Best. 1997. A 2-year longitudinal analysis of the relationships between violent assault and substance use in women. *Journal of Consulting and Clinical Psychology* 65:835–47.

Kirkwood, Catherine. 1993. *Leaving Abusive Partners.* Thousand Oaks, CA: Sage.

Krishnan, Satya P., Judith C. Hilbert, and Dawn Van Leeuwen. 2001. Domestic violence and help-seeking behaviors among rural women: Results from a shelter-based study. *Family and Community Health* 24:28–38.

Kuhn, Randall, and Dennis P. Culhane. 1998. Applying cluster analysis to test a typology of homelessness by pattern of shelter utilization: Results from the analysis of administrative data. *American Journal of Community Psychology* 26, no. 2:207–32.

Kusmer, Kenneth L. 2002. *Down and Out, On the Road: The Homeless in American History.* Oxford: Oxford University Press.

Kvall, James. 2008. *The Economic Imperative for Health Reform.* Washington: Center for American Progress. http:www.americanprogress.org/issues/2008/12/pdf/health_imperative.pdf (accessed on March 23, 2009).

Lee, Barrett A., and Christopher J. Schreck. 2005. Danger on the streets: Marginality and victimization among homeless people. *American Behavioral Scientist* 48:1055–81.

Lindsay-Blue, Denise. 1999. A comparative study of reported parenting practices in abused and nonabused shelter populations of women. Ph.D. diss., Alliant University.

Lynch, James P. 1987. Routine activity and victimization at work. *Journal of Quantitative Criminology* 3:283–300.

Lyons, Linda. 2005. Nation's hunger, homelessness trouble Americans. *Public Opinion* 12:133–34.

Madriz, Esther. 1997. *Nothing Bad Happens to Good Girls: Fear of Crime in Women's Lives*. Berkeley: University of California Press.

Martin, Del. 1976. *Battered Wives*. San Francisco: Glide.

Martin, Emily. 1992. *The Woman in the Body*. Boston: Beacon.

Maslow, Abraham H. 1943. A theory of human motivation. *Psychological Review* 50: 370–96.

Maston, Cathy, and Patsy Klaus. 2005. *Criminal Victimization in the United States, 2003: Statistical Tables*. Washington: U.S. Department of Justice.

McLellan, A. Thomas., Harvey Kushner, David Metzger, Roger Peters, Iris Smith, Grant Grissom, Helen Pettinati, and Milton Argeriou. 1992. The fifth edition of the Addiction Severity Index. *Journal of Substance Abuse Treatment* 9:199–213.

Metraux, Stephen, and Dennis P. Culhane. 1999. Family dynamics, housing and recurring homelessness among women in New York City shelters. *Journal of Family Issues* 20:371–96.

Meyers, Marian. 1997. *News Coverage of Violence against Women: Engendering Blame*. Thousand Oaks, CA: Sage.

Miethe, Terance, and Robert Meier. 1990. Opportunity, choice, and criminal victimization: A test of a theoretical model. *Journal of Research in Crime and Delinquency* 27:243–66.

Miller, Alison B., and Michael B. Keys. 2001. Understanding dignity in the lives of homeless persons. *American Journal of Community Psychology* 29:331–54.

Miller, Jody, and Norman A. White. 2004. Situational effects of gender inequality on girls' participation in violence. In *Girls' Violence: Myths and Realities*, edited by C. Alder and A. Worrall, 167–90. Albany: State University of New York Press.

Mustaine, Elizabeth Ehrhardt, and Richard A. Tewksbury. 1997a. Obstacles in the assessment of routine activity theory. *Social Pathology* 3:177–94.

———. 1997b. The risk of victimization in the workplace for men and women. *Humanity and Society* 21, no. 1:17–38.

National Center on Family Homelessness. 2004. *Violence in the Lives of Homeless Women*. Newton Centre, MA: National Center on Family Homelessness.

National Coalition for the Homeless. 2008. Domestic violence and homelessness. NCH Fact Sheet #7. http://www.nationalhomeless.org/factsheets/domestic.html (accessed September 2, 2009).

———. 2009. *Hate, Violence, and Death on Main Street USA: A Report on Hate Crimes and Violence against People Experiencing Homelessness 2008*. http://www.national

homeless.org/publications/hatecrimes/hate_report_2008.pdf (accessed September 22, 2009).

National Law Center on Homelessness and Poverty and the National Coalition for the Homeless. 2009. *Homes Not Handcuffs: The Criminalization of Homelessness in U.S. Cities.* http://www.nationalhomeless.org/publications/crimreport/index.html (accessed September 5, 2009).

National Network to End Domestic Violence. 2008. *Domestic Violence Counts 2008: A 24- Hour Census of Domestic Violence Shelters and Services.* http://www.nnedv.org/docs/Census/DVCounts2008/DVCounts08_Report_Color.pdf (accessed September 16, 2009).

National Research Council. 1996. *Understanding Violence against Women.* Washington: National Academy Press.

Noll, Jennie G. 2005. Does childhood sexual abuse set in motion a cycle of violence against women? *Journal of Interpersonal Violence* 20:455–62.

North, Carol S., Karin Eyrich, David Pollio, and Edward L. Spitznagel, 2004. Are rates of psychiatric disorders in the homeless population changing? *American Journal of Public Health* 94:103–8.

North, Carol S., Elizabeth M. Smith, Edward L. Spitznagel. 1994. Violence and the homeless: An epidemiologic study of victimization and aggression. *Journal of Traumatic Stress* 7:95–110.

North, Carol S., Sanna J. Thompson, Elizabeth M. Smith, and Linda M. Kyburz. 1996. Violence in the lives of homeless mothers in a substance abuse treatment program: A descriptive study. *Journal of Interpersonal Violence* 11:234–49.

O'Connell, James J. 2005. *Premature Mortality in Homeless Populations: A Review of the Literature.* Nashville, TN: National Health Care for the Homeless Council, Inc.

Padgett, Deborah K., and E. L. Struening. 1992. Victimization and traumatic injuries among the homeless: Associations with alcohol, drug, and mental problems. *American Journal of Orthopsychiatry* 62:525–34.

Parker, Linda. S. 1997. A "brutal case" or "only a family jar"? Violence against women in San Diego County, 1880–1900. *Violence against Women* 3:294–318.

Pettiway, Leon E. 1997. *Workin' It: Women Living through Drugs and Crime.* Philadelphia: Temple University Press.

Potter, Hillary. 2006. An argument for black feminist criminology: Understanding African American women's experiences with intimate partner abuse using an integrated approach. *Feminist Criminology* 1:106–24.

Raphael, Jody. 2000. *Saving Bernice: Battered Women, Welfare and Poverty.* Boston: Northeastern University Press.

———. 2004. *Listening to Olivia: Violence, Poverty and Prostitution.* Boston: Northeastern University Press.

——— and Deborah Shapiro. 2001. *Sisters Speak Out: The Lives and Needs of Prostituted Women in Chicago—A Research Study.* Chicago: Center for Impact Research.

Rasche, Christine. 1988. Minority women and domestic violence: The unique dilemmas of battered women of color. *Journal of Contemporary Criminal Justice* 4:150–71.

Reinharz, Shulamit. 1992. *Feminist Methods in Social Research.* New York: Oxford University Press.

Richie, Beth E. 1996. *Compelled to Crime: The Gender Entrapment of Battered Black Women.* New York: Routledge.

Roberts, Steven V. Reagan on homelessness: Many choose to live in the streets. *The New York Times,* December 23, 1988.

Rodgers, Karen, and Georgia Roberts. 1995. Women's non-spousal multiple victimization: A test of the routine activities theory. *Canadian Journal of Criminology* 37:361–91.

Roll, Carolyn N., Paul A. Toro, and Gina L. Ortola. 1999. Characteristics and experiences of homeless adults: A comparison of single men, single women and women with children. *Journal of Community Psychology* 27:189–98.

Salomon, Amy, Ellen Bassuk, and Nick Huntington. 2002. The relationship between intimate partner violence and the use of addictive substances in poor and homeless single mothers. *Violence against Women* 8:785–815.

Schaff, Kristin K., and Thomas R. McCane. 1998. Relationship of childhood sexual, physical and combined sexual and physical abuse to adult victimization and posttraumatic stress disorder. *Child Abuse and Neglect* 22:1119–33.

Schecter, Susan. 1982. *Woman and Male Violence: The Visions and Struggles of the Battered Women's Movement.* Boston: South End.

Schwartz, Martin D., Walter S. DeKeseredy, David Tait, and Shahid Alvi. 2001. Male peer support and a feminist routine activities theory: Understanding sexual assault on the college campus. *Justice Quarterly* 18:623–49.

Schwartz, Martin D., and Victoria L. Pitts. 1995. Exploring a feminist routine activities approach to explaining sexual assault. *Justice Quarterly* 12:9–31.

Seltser, Barry J., and Donald E. Miller. 1993. *Homeless Families and the Struggle for Dignity.* Urbana: University of Illinois Press.

Silbert, Mimi H., and Ayala M. Pines. 1981. Sexual abuse as an antecedent to prostitution. *Child Abuse and Neglect* 5:407–11.

Silver, Gillian, and Rea Panares. 2000. *The Health of Homeless Women: Information for State Maternal and Child Health Programs.* Washington: U.S. Department of Health and Human Services, Maternal and Child Health Bureau of the Health Resources and Services Administration.

Simons, Ronald, and Les B. Whitbeck. 1991. Sexual abuse as a precursor to prostitution and victimization among adolescent and adult homeless women. *Family Issues* 12:361–79.

Smith, Alisa. 2000. It's my decision, isn't it? A research note on battered women's perceptions of mandatory intervention laws. *Violence against Women* 6:1384–1402.

Smith, Meredith Y., Bruce D. Rapkin, Gary Winkel, Carolyn Springer, Rosy Chabara, and Ira S. Feldman. 2000. Housing status and health care service utilization among low-income persons with HIV/AIDS. *Journal of General Internal Medicine* 15:731–38.

Snow, David A., and Leon Anderson. 1993. *Down on Their Luck: A Study of Homeless Street People.* Berkeley: University of California Press.

Snow, David A., Susan G. Baker, and Leon Anderson. 1989. Criminality and homeless men: An empirical assessment. *Social Problems* 36:532–49.

Snyder, Howard N. 2000. *Sexual Assault of Young Children as Reported to Law Enforcement: Victim, Incident and Offender Characteristics.* Washington: U.S. Department of Justice, Bureau of Justice Statistics.

Spitzer, Stephen. 1975. Toward a Marxian theory of deviance. *Social Problems* 22:638–51.

Stack, Carol B. 1974. *All Our Kin: Strategies for Survival in a Black Community.* New York: Basic.

Stanko, Elizabeth A. 1990. *Everyday Violence: How Women and Men Experience Sexual and Physical Danger.* San Francisco: HarperCollins.

————. 1993. Ordinary fear: Women, violence, and personal safety. In *Violence against Women: The Bloody Footprints*, edited by P. B. Bart and E. G. Moran, 155–64. Thousand Oaks, CA: Sage.

Stein, Judith A., and Lillian Gelberg. 1995. Gender differences in the mediating effect of substance abuse on the severity of homelessness. *Experimental and Clinical Psychopharmacology* 3:75–86.

Steinbock, Marcia R. 1995. Homeless female headed families: Relationships at risk. *Marriage and Family Review* 20:143–59.

Stephens, B. Joyce, and Peter G. Sinden. 2000. Victims' voices: Domestic assault victims' perceptions of police demeanor. *Journal of Interpersonal Violence* 15:534–47.

Stergiopoulos, Vicky, and Nathan Herrmann. 2003. Old and homeless: A review and survey of older adults who use shelters in an urban setting. *Canadian Journal of Psychiatry* 48:374–80.

Straus, Murray A. 1979. Measuring intrafamily conflict and violence: The Conflict Tactics Scale. *Journal of Marriage and the Family* 41:75–88.

———— and Richard J. Gelles. 1990. Societal change and change in family violence from 1975 to 1985 as revealed by two national surveys. In *Physical Violence in*

American Families, edited by Murray A. Straus and Richard J. Gelles, 113–31. New Brunswick, NJ: Transaction.

———— and Suzanne K. Steinmetz. 1980. *Behind Closed Doors: Violence in the American Family*. Garden City, NY: Anchor.

Sweet, Nova, and Richard Tewksbury. 2000. What's a nice girl like you doing in a place like this? Pathways to a career in stripping. *Sociological Spectrum* 20:325–43.

Tjaden, Patricia, and Nancy Thoennes. 1998. Prevalence, incidence, and consequences of violence against women: Findings from the National Violence Against Women Survey. National Institute of Justice Research in Brief, http://www.ncjrs.gov/pdffiles/172837.pdf (accessed September 15, 2009).

————. 1999. *Violence and Threats of Violence against Women and Men in the United States, 1994–1996*. Ann Arbor, MI: Inter-University Consortium for Political and Social Research.

————. 2000. *Full Report of the Prevalence, Incidence, and Consequences of Violence against Women: Findings from the National Violence Against Women Survey*. Washington: National Institute of Justice and the Centers for Disease Control and Prevention.

Tyler, Kimberly A., and Ana M. Cauce. 2002. Perpetrators of early physical and sexual abuse among homeless and runaway adolescents. *Child Abuse and Neglect* 26:1261–74.

Tyler, Kimberly A., Dan R. Hoyt, and Les B. Whitbeck. 2000. The effects of early sexual abuse on later sexual victimization among female homeless and runaway adolescents. *Journal of Interpersonal Violence* 15:235–51.

———— and Ana M. Cauce. 2001. The effects of a high-risk environment on the sexual victimization of homeless and runaway youth. *Violence and Victims* 16:441–55.

U.S. Conference of Mayors. 1998. *A Status Report on Hunger and Homelessness in America's Cities*. Washington: U.S. Conference of Mayors.

————. 2008. *A Status Report on Hunger and Homelessness*. Washington: U.S. Conference of Mayors.

Valentine, Gil. 1992. Images of danger: Women's sources of information about the spatial distribution of male violence. *Area* 24:22–29.

Walker, Robert, T. K. Logan, Carol E. Jordan, and Jacquelyn C. Campbell. 2004. An integrative review of separation in the context of victimization: Consequences and implications for women. *Trauma, Violence and Abuse* 5:143–93.

Wenzel, Suzanne L., Paul Koegel, and Lillian Gelberg. 2000. Antecedents of physical and sexual victimization among homeless women: A comparison to homeless men. *American Journal of Community Psychology* 28:367–90.

Wenzel, Suzanne L., Barbara D. Leake, and Lillian Gelberg. 2001. Risk factors for major violence among homeless women. *Journal of Interpersonal Violence* 16: 739–52.

Wesely, Jennifer K. 2002. Growing up sexualized: Issues of power and violence in the lives of female exotic dancers. *Violence against Women* 8:1182–1207.

———. 2006. Considering the context of women's violence: Gender, lived experiences and cumulative victimization. *Feminist Criminology* 1:303–28.

———. 2009. Mom said we had a money-maker: Sexualization and survival contexts among homeless women. *Symbolic Interaction* 32:91–105.

Whitbeck, Les B., and Dan R. Hoyt. 1999. *Nowhere to Grow: Homeless and Runaway Adolescents and Their Families*. Hawthorne, NY: Aldine de Gruyter.

———. 2002. "Midwest Longitudinal Study of Homeless Adolescents." Unpublished technical report.

———, Yoder, K.A., Anna M. Cauce, and Matt Paradise. 2001. Deviant behavior and victimization among homeless and runaway adolescents. *Journal of Interpersonal Violence* 16:1175–1204.

Whitbeck, Les B., and Ronald L. Simons. 1990. Life on the streets: The victimization of runaway and homeless adolescents. *Youth and Society* 22:108–25.

Widom, Catherine S. 1989a. The cycle of violence. *Science* 244:160–66.

———. 1989b. Child abuse, neglect and adult behavior: Research design and findings on criminality, violence and child abuse. *American Journal of Orthopsychiatry* 59:355–67.

———. 1989c. Does violence beget violence? A critical examination of the literature. *Psychological Bulletin* 106:3–28.

———. 1992. *The Cycle of Violence*. Washington: U.S. Department of Justice, National Institute of Justice.

———. 2000. Motivations and mechanisms in the "cycle of violence." In *Motivation and Child Maltreatment*, edited by D. J. Hansen, 1–38. Lincoln: University of Nebraska Press.

Wilder Research Center. 1998. *Minnesota Statewide Survey of Persons without Permanent Shelter*. Vol. 1: *Adults and Their Children*. St. Paul, MN: Wilder Research Center.

Wolak, Janis, and David Finkelhor. 1998. Children exposed to partner violence. In *Partner Violence: A Comprehensive Review of 20 Years of Research*, edited by Jana L. Jasinski and Linda M. Williams, 73–112. Thousand Oaks, CA: Sage.

Wood, David, R. Burciaga Valdez, Toshi Hayashi, and Albert Shen. 1990. Homeless and housed families in Los Angeles: A study comparing demographic, economic, and family function characteristics. *American Journal of Public Health* 80:1049–52.

Wooldredge, John D., Francis T. Cullen, and Edward J. Latessa. 1992. Research note: Victimization in the workplace; A test of routine activities theory. *Justice Quarterly* 9:325–35.

Worden, Alissa P., and Bonnie E. Carlson. 2005. Attitudes and beliefs about domestic violence: Results of a public opinion survey: Beliefs about causes. *Journal of Interpersonal Violence* 20:1219–43.

Wright, James D. 1988. *Address Unknown: The Homeless in America*. Hawthorne, NY: Aldine de Gruyter.

——— and Joel A. Devine. 1993. Family backgrounds and the substance-abusive homeless: The New Orleans experience. *Community Psychologist* 26:35–37.

——— and Neil Eddington. 1993. The New Orleans Homeless Substance Abusers Program. *Alcoholism Treatment Quarterly* 10:51–64.

Wright, James D., Joel A. Devine, and Laurie Joyner. 1993. *The Least of Mine: The New Orleans Homeless Substance Abusers Project Final Report: Final Report to the National Institute of Alcohol Abuse and Alcoholism*. Washington: National Institute of Alcohol Abuse and Alcoholism

Wright, James D., and Amy M. Donley. 2008. Lovely, dark, and deep: Homeless people living in the woods in Orlando. Paper presented at the second annual Florida Homeless and Supportive Housing Conference, Orlando.

——— and Tracy L. Dietz. 2008. Elderly homelessness: A growing concern. In *Homelessness in America*, edited by Robert McNamara, 1:175–88. New York: Greenwood.

Wright, James D., Beth Rubin, and Joel A. Devine. 1998. *Beside the Golden Door: Policy, Politics and the Homeless*. Hawthorne, NY: Aldine de Gruyter.

Wright, James D., and Eleanor Weber. 1987. *Homelessness and Health*.Washington: McGraw-Hill.

Index